PUBLIC ADMINISTRATION DESK BOOK

D0170455

James R. Coleman
and
Robert E. Dugan

Z
7164
.A2
C59
1990

GOVERNMENT RESEARCH PUBLICATIONS

GOVERNMENT RESEARCH PUBLICATIONS, INC.
BOX 122
NEWTON, MA 02159-0122
(617)244-9046

Library of Congress Cataloging-in-Publication Data

Coleman, James R., 1933-
    Public administration desk book / by James R. Coleman & Robert E.
Dugan.

    Includes bibliographical references.
    ISBN 0-931684-12-9 :
    1. Reference books--Public administration. 2. Public
administration--Bibliography. 3. Public administration--United
States--Bibliography. 4. United States--Politics and government-
-Bibliography. I. Dugan, Robert E., 1952- . II. Title.
Z7164.A2C59 1990
[JK421]
016.35--dc20   90-32809
                                                         CIP

ISBN 0-931684-12-9
Copyright 1990
by Government Research Publications, Inc.

Design and typesetting by *FAST TYPE, Inc.*

Printing by D.S. Graphics, Pepperel, MA. This book was printed on a Miehle 40" Perfecta and bound in house.

ACKNOWLEDGEMENTS

We wish to thank our colleagues at the Sawyer Library and the Mugar Law Library of Suffolk University, the State Library of the Commonwealth of Massachusetts, the State Library of New York, the Library of Congress and elsewhere. Their assistance comes as a routine feature of their invaluable profession but we are nonetheless grateful. We particularly benefited from assistance and suggestions from Edward Bander, a law librarian, and David Pfeiffer, who is not a librarian but might well be. Both are at Suffolk University and we thank them also.

Several people read typescript of this Desk Book and provided valuable suggestions, corrections or encouragement; for this we thank Patricia Ahearn, James V. Brewin, Jr., Catherine M. Merlo, Karen P. Walsh and A. John Vogt. And for their labor on the typescript we thank Karen P. Walsh and Alethea Small.

In one of those rare, gracious contributions, Joan A. Casey of the Advisory Commission on Intergovernmental Relations read our manuscript and made a great many corrections, additions and suggestions which were immediately right. For her, especially, we wish that this Desk Book could have been impossibly complete, absolutely correct and perfect in judgment. That would be our thanks to her. It is entirely our fault that it is not.

It is impossible to develop a resource such as this in a short time without advice from others whose opinion we respect. Of all of these people, we are most grateful to Don Levitan who first inspired and then advised, prodded, criticized, praised us through the effort. We suspect that Evelyn Levitan does the same for him.

Both of us have been involved for many years in assisting students and those employed by public agencies in finding and organizing information. Their inquiries have guided the organization of this book. With its orientation toward ease of use, it is dedicated to them.

CONTENTS

Acknowledgements   iii

About the Authors   ix

Preface   xi

How to Use This Book   xiii

PART 1:   PEOPLE, THEIR OFFICES AND AGENCIES   . . .   1

    I. Directories   3

        A. General Directories   3

        B. Federal Directories   5

        C. State Directories   10

        D. Local Directories   13

    II. Guides to Activities   15

        A. Current Activities   15

        B. General and Historical Activities   17

   III. Directories of those Influencing
       Government   19

        A. Consultants   19

        B. Lobbyists and Legal Counsel   21

        C. Others   23

vi

PART 2: STATISTICS 27

   I. Guides to Statistics Sources 29

      A. Directories 29

      B. Indexes and Abstracts 32

      C. Statistical Policy 35

      D. Statistics Announcement Periodicals . . . 36

      E. Guides to Online Statistical Databases
         and Services 36

   II. General Statistics Sources 39

   III. Finance and Government Operations
      Statistics 43

      A. Financial Statistics 43

      B. Budget, Accounting and
         Auditing Information 47

   IV. Economic, Business and Labor Statistics . . 49

   V. Voting Statistics 54

   VI. Public Opinion Data 55

**PART 3: TERMS, RESEARCH METHODS
AND PUBLISHING** 57

   I. Dictionaries and Handbooks 59

   II. Research Methods 63

      A. General Reference Tools 63

      B. Grant Reference Tools 65

      C. Library Research Tools 68

      D. Research Centers 70

      E. Libraries 70

   III. Publishing 72

      A. Non-governmental Publishing 72

      B. Federal Publishing 74

      C. State Publishing 80

      D. Municipal Publishing 84

PART 4: PUBLIC ADMINISTRATION PERIODICALS 87

    I. Abstracting Services 89

    II. Indexing Services 96

    III. Selected Public Administration
        Periodicals 101

    IV. Directories of Periodicals 133

**PART 5: ONLINE AND
        OTHER MACHINE-BASED SERVICES** 135

    I. Introduction 137

    II. Recommendations 139

    III. Database Vendors 140

    IV. Additional Databases of Special Interest
        in Public Administration 145

        A. Demographic Data 145

        B. Federal Government Activities and
           Publications 147

        C. Law Services 150

        D. News Databases 151

    V. CD-ROM and Other Non-Online Sources
        of Machine-Readable Information 152

        A. On CD-ROM 152

           1. Introduction 152

           2. Some CD-ROM Products and
              Vendors 154

           3. Sources of Information 155

        B. Data on Diskettes 156

        C. Magnetic Tapes 157

    VI. Directories and Other Sources of
        Information 160

viii

PART 6: LAW AND REGULATORY REPORTER SERVICES 163

   I. Reporter Services and their Uses: Introduction 165

   II. Law Libraries: Introduction 166

   III. A Selection for the Public Administrator . . . 168

   IV. Major Publishers 183

PART 7: ASSOCIATIONS AND INSTITUTES 185

   I. Directories 187

   II. A Selection of Organizations 189

APPENDIX A: A Basic Library 205

APPENDIX B: Other Guides to Public Administration Information 213

TITLE INDEX 223

SUBJECT INDEX 235

About the Authors

James R. Coleman is Assistant Director and head of public services at the Sawyer Library of Suffolk University. Prior to his career as a librarian he taught at universities in the South and in New England. He has published articles on legal information sources, on microcomputers and on new library technology. Coleman holds masters degrees in library science and in English literary history.

Robert E. Dugan is the Delaware State Librarian. Prior to this position he was Research Associate for the U.S. National Commission on Libraries and Information Science. Prior to his federal service, Dugan worked in a state library administrative agency, as a library director, and as a reference librarian. He has published articles on statistics, library automation, library services to the deaf and urban history. Dugan holds masters degrees in library science and public administration.

PREFACE

This book is for practitioners, researchers and students of American Public Administration. Our purpose is to simplify finding needed information.

Where most guides to the literature of Public Administration direct attention to specialized studies or articles on aspects of this diverse field, we concentrate on directing you to the reference tools that serve the field and the practitioner. Here you will find the indexes, the statistical sources, the handbooks and encyclopedias, the loose-leaf services and online files, the professional association publications and directories. They are the *See These First* tools of Public Administration as a profession and a field of study. If there is a short cut from where-you-are to the information you need, we have tried to identify it for you. We also direct you to tools that will allow you to survey the many books and the thousands of articles written each year on Public Administration.

This is a *Desk Book*. It will fit within a briefcase and serve to guide those who consult it to the reference resources of the special libraries consulted by the practitioner, and to some of the resources of law libraries, as well as to the resources of large public and university libraries.

Our *Desk Book* is provided with a thorough subject index which gives, under subject headings, the title and document type of tools on each subject. In many instances, consulting the index will be all that is required. There is also a name and title index.

We believe this *Desk Book* will be a useful addition to the briefcase and the desk of any student, practitioner, professor or researcher. With it they can identify, at minimum, the reference tools and information sources they need to consult or, as often happens, those they will need to refer to when calling a library or sending an assistant to search out information. However, there are important things that this *Desk Book* is not. It will not serve all the needs of the academic researcher. It does not cover international or comparative Public Administration or the history of Public Administration. It is almost entirely a guide to reference tools for current Public Administration as practiced in the United States.

For the student in Public Administration programs throughout the country we intend that this book provide a key to the practical tools of their field: the periodicals, indexes, online services, the data sources, the legal reporters, sources of financial, personnel, health and management information, the key public administration association publications.

HOW TO USE THIS BOOK

Please examine the Table of Contents first. This *Desk Book* is not an "unfolding story" of Public Administration, that is, first a history, then theories, then federal or constitutional matters, etc. It is a guide to the reference tools of contemporary public administration as practiced in the United States. We expect you to go to the section you need, find some guidance to information sources, perhaps take some notes, and put it aside.

Look next at the indexes. The Subject Index is most important. In the Subject Index we have included the titles of reference books, journals, online and loose-leaf services (which appear capitalized along with the law library location number) dealing with each subject. We expect that in many instances all you will need to consult is this Subject Index. You might turn to the indicated pages of the guide only if sources named in the index are not available to you and you need a substitute. Much information necessary in Public Administration such as statistical data and the names of agencies and individuals is found in a number of sources. In addition, there is an index which gives the page references for each title and name.

With each part of the *Desk Book* introductory paragraphs describe the tools for the topic and present those judgments about methods of research we have come to feel are sound. Our judgments may harm one or two commodities in the information industry, but they will not, we are confident, harm the user and may save them considerable time, frustration and, last of all, money.

Following the introduction to each section is a rational and obvious organization of references to sources of information, how to locate them, and annotations on their use.

So, that is the way we have done it: broad, general pointers, perhaps some judgments on how to proceed, then specific arrows to the target. Use of the Subject Index alone gives you another, quicker access.

Appendix A provides a "basic survival library," a brief list of reference tools which we regard as the minimum essential titles in any library serving Public Administration information requirements. In Appendix B we describe other guides to Public Administration information, bibliographies, etc. Several other guides have much to recommend them. Usually they will cover, often with very useful annotations, public administration treatises and articles which we do not mention since we concentrate on reference tools.

In behalf of our emphasis on the Public Administration practitioner—the administrator of an agency, not-for-profit, or bureau, the person in the department who knows *where to find the information*, the administrative assistant who goes for information—we believe that our approach is an excellent way to introduce you to new sources, new technology, new methods. As a desk book or in the briefcase, this book should ease and improve your search for information and provide a great many shortcuts to the familiar goals. Our experience is that students and researchers have information goals which are similar to those of the practitioner, and similar time constraints as well.

A final word. Learn by doing. Take this *Public Administration Desk Book* along on your next pursuit of information, or have it on your desk for when you next call around or send someone for information. Information, in its many modern forms, remains an enigma to those who read about but do not use it. Above all, use our book to avoid that common student mistake of behaving as if information came only from periodical articles and books you could check out from your library. This preconception misses all the shortcuts employed by researchers and information professionals: the abstracting services, the loose-leafs, the excellent summaries of most any topic of public interest, the guides, directories, etc. This poor practice originates with those who believe that the "discipline" of chasing journal articles and carrying books home from the library is good for students. If that means that their students fail to use the professional information resources and short cuts of a good reference library, we do not agree.

PUBLIC ADMINISTRATION DESK BOOK

Part 1
PEOPLE, THEIR OFFICES AND AGENCIES

Part 1 of this *Desk Book* is a guide to directories and information about people in and around federal, state and local government. Most practicing public administrators depend upon other public administrators and specialists to provide the information they need. It is not possible to cite all the directories of all the specialists a public administrator may need in their work: engineers, health care providers, environmentalists, etc. However, we have cited the sources which identify public administrators, elected officials and a great many others who can assist on a wide range of issues. Also you will find here the directories to the membership organizations and firms that put you in contact with people.

All of the annotations were derived from reviewing and using the sources cited. All the directories were found in state, public and academic libraries. For the public administrator, the libraries of the United States provide a comprehensive system in which to locate these resources and information. The library you use may not have all of the resources cited in this *Desk Book*; however, libraries of all types communicate among themselves to share resources and information. We recommend that the starting place of any information seeking effort begin at a local library. Directories of libraries and guides to using the library are included in Part 3 of this *Desk Book*.

Contact by phone is, of course, an important method of securing information for those who know precisely what information they are seeking, and many of the directories listed here include telephone numbers. Also remember that the Blue Pages of the telephone directories for state capitols provide the most current government telephone numbers and that Yellow Pages will identify associations, publishers and many special interest groups. These days most Yellow Pages have subject indexes. The blue pages in the District of Columbia directory gives an alphabetical organization of federal government departments and offices and provides several thousand specific phone numbers, for instance, numbers for each judicial office in the federal district court, thirty-five offices in the Federal Communications Commission, etc. Each department has a general information number with which you can reach a staff member who will search a special directory for the individual or exact office you seek.

I. DIRECTORIES

This section is devoted to the major directories identifying public administrators and elected officials on the federal, state and local levels. The major directories of elected officials and their staff are presented in this section. Those working in government have a responsibility to assist those they represent; therefore, a public administrator or researcher should not be shy about contacting an official agency to seek assistance.

A. GENERAL DIRECTORIES

These are resources which include more than one level of government, or identify those influencing government.

Almanac of American Politics

Washington, DC: National Journal, 1989. Biennial.

The main body of this work is an examination of each state's political status, a short history and a narrative concerning the current governor, congressional representatives and presidential politics. Statistics are provided on the state population, the state share of federal tax burden and expenditure and on recent presidential elections. Each member of Congress is discussed; and ratings by several national associations are given. Information on their campaign funding is also included. Each congressional representative's district is examined in a narrative preceding the numeric data. Senate and House committees and subcommittees and their members are listed near the end of this work. Following the section on committees is a statistical section on demographics including several comparative charts ranking states. Another section reviews campaign finances and provides charts on the top ten fund raisers by chamber and the financial activity of the two major party organizations. A comprehensive combined personal name and subject index completes the work.

Federal-State-Local Government Directory

Washington, DC: Braddock Communications, 1987.

A comprehensive directory of officials from the federal executive, legislative and judiciary branches, along with its related agencies and committees. Also included are national and state political committees and organizations, selected news media and public policy organizations. State information identifies majority party legislative leadership, state and local governmental organizations and includes biographies on chief state officials such as the governor. This tool is an important starting place when searching for information such as an address for a federal agency, congressional telephone numbers, or sources of statistical information. Citations identify the governmental official and provide an address and telephone number when appropriate. Although a general subject index is included, we recommended that the Tables of Contents be used when searching.

Taylor's Encyclopedia of Government Officials; Federal and State

Volume XI, 1987-1988. Dallas, TX: Political Research, Inc., 1987. Biennial.

This work has become a standard reference on federal and state government held by most public libraries. The work identifies key officials in the federal executive, legislative and judicial branches. It includes photographs of selected officials. State profiles include a readable map of congressional districts, photographs of elected state officials and the congressional delegation, lists of members of the legislature and the state judiciary, and other facts such as population, motto and state seal. A personal name index is included.

Washington Information Directory

Washington, DC: Congressional Quarterly, 1988-89. Biennial.

Since 1975 this has become an valuable guide to identifying federal government departments and agencies, Congress and non-governmental organizations. Main chapters are divided along subject areas closely resembling the executive departments. Each subject is further narrowed into sub-fields; and then agencies, congressional committees and non-governmental organizations are identified and briefly described. Although descriptions are brief, the annotation is adequate to learn what the office does and provide contact information.

There are several reference lists including:

foreign embassies and U.S. Ambassadors;

elected executive officials of state government;

major labor unions; mayors of cities of 75,000 people or more;

regional federal information sources arranged by federal departments;

addresses of members of Congress; and

House and Senate committees.

Indexes are arranged by personal name and by subject.

B. FEDERAL DIRECTORIES

Congressional Directory

Washington, DC: Government Printing Office, 1989. Biennial.

This official congressional directory is compiled biennially by congressional session. This is not the easiest tool to use, but there is a wealth of useful information. Biographic information on all members of Congress is included, along with lists for State delegations, office numbers, terms of service and committee membership.

Congressional district maps are also included. Briefer directory information is included for the executive office and its many department and independent agencies, the judiciary, international organizations, foreign diplomatic representatives and consular offices in the United States and a listing of what seems to be all of the possible press galleries (news press, photographers, radio and television, periodical press, etc.).

The abridged and the full Table of Contents is in alphabetical order rather than in page order and serves as a subject index. An individual name index is also included.

Congressional Staff Directory

30th ed. Mount Vernon, VA: Congressional Staff Directory, Ltd., 1988. Biennial.

This volume includes brief biographical information for approximately 3,200 congressional staff members. It identifies key members of each congressional office, congressional committee and support agency. Committee assignments, election results and addresses of state offices for each congressional member are also provided. Indexes are included for key word, subject and personal name.

Congressional Yellow Book

Washington, DC: Monitor Publishing Company. 1988. Loose-leaf, updated quarterly.

This is a comprehensive quarterly guide which identifies and provides descriptive information concerning congressional officials, administrators and functions. It begins with a collection of state maps showing congressional districts, most large enough to include counties and in some cases, municipalities. Each senator and representative is profiled. Profiles include the individual's photograph, basic personal data and identifies key staff aides, committee assignments, other positions within the Congress or affiliated political party and addresses of their state offices.

Extensive details found in few other resources are included on congressional committees. Information identifies the committee's address, jurisdiction, members, key staff aides and subcommittees. Congressional support agencies such as the Congressional Budget Office, Government Printing Office and Library of Congress are described in some detail and key administrators are identified.

Encyclopedia of Governmental Advisory Organizations 1990-91

7th ed. Detroit, MI: Gale Research Company, 1989.

This resource describes over 5,400 active and inactive advisory committees, commissions and boards to the federal government. The directory is organized into ten subject sections with committees organized alphabetically according to a key word in the title of the committee, such as "Aging", or by the primary purpose of the committee so that the "Advisory Committee on Older Americans" appears with other committees involved with "aging." Each entry includes an address, history and authority, program, membership, staff publications and reports and meeting information.

There are several useful indexes: personnel; titles of reports and publications by committees; organizations arranged by the federal department jurisdiction; subject/title/key word index. As with several Gale Research Company publications there is a periodic updating publication *New Governmental Advisory Organizations*

Federal Executive Directory

Washington, DC: Carroll Publishing Company, 1989. Bimonthly.

This directory identifies nearly 90,000 key federal executives. The first section indexes personal names. A second section is arranged by executive department, further divided into sub-departments and bureaus, and for each executive position provides the address, lists the position title, identifies the incumbent and includes a telephone number. Similar information concerning members of Congress, congressional committees and subcommittees, Congressional agencies and congressional staff is found in the third section. The keyword index is also useful. Carroll Publishing Company (not currently listed in the publisher directory of *Books in Print*) is located at 1058 Thomas Jefferson St., Washington, DC 20007, (202)333-8620.

Federal Regulatory Directory

5th ed. Washington, DC: Congressional Quarterly, Inc., 1986.

This directory describes the major regulatory agencies of the federal government. Information on each of the major agencies includes descriptions about their responsibilities, background, powers and authority, administrators or commissioners, the departments in the organization including names of administrators and telephone numbers and functions, location of regional offices if any, sources of departmental or agency information and relationship to congressional committees and legislation. There is also a bibliography of published external information sources concerning the agency's activities. The Directory also includes less complete information on other departments and agencies which are considered less regulatory in nature.

Also useful is the Appendix which includes an article on how to use the *Federal Register* and the *Code of Federal Regulations* as well as the text of several acts and executive orders including the Paperwork Reduction Act. There are separate personal name and subject indexes.

Federal Staff Directory

Mt. Vernon, VA: Congressional Staff Directory, Ltd., 1989. Annual.

This directory identifies some 28,000 executives and staff members of the executive office and its agencies, the executive departments, independent agencies and quasi-official international and non-government organizations. Citations provide addresses and telephone numbers. In addition, the directory includes biographical information on 2,400 key executives. There is a index of personnel and a key word subject index to facilitate access.

Federal Yellow Book

Washington, DC: Monitor Publishing Company, 1988. Looseleaf, updated quarterly.

This publication is important because of its updating. It identifies some 31,000 officials and administrators in the executive branch of the federal government. The directory is arranged, first, by the various units and sub-units of the Office of the President and Office of the Vice President, then the executive departments, and then the independent agencies. No information is provided beyond identifying the official and providing an address and telephone number. Regional offices of the departments and agencies are also identified. The index is arranged alphabetically by agency.

Politics in America

Washington, DC: Congressional Quarterly, Inc., 1989. Biennial.

This resource provides information on each of the members of the congressional delegation from each state. The profiles go well beyond what you find in directories. They give the usual personal data and a photograph; they also include a detailed discussion of the individual's position within Washington's political community and in their home state. A table indicates the member's committee assignments, last election statistics, campaign finances, and an analysis of their voting records in terms of key issues, presidential support, party unity and selected special interest group ratings. A brief description of their districts are included with profiles of members of the House of Representatives.

United States Government Manual 1988/89

Washington, DC: Office of the Federal Register
National Archives and Records Administration,
1988. Annual.

This official handbook of the federal government provides comprehensive information on the agencies of the legislative, judicial and executive branches, including citations for enabling legislation or authority, primary functions, responsibilities and identifying key officials. Organizational charts are also included. The manual includes information on the quasi-official agencies, international organizations in which the United States participates, boards, committees and commissions.

Useful appendices include commonly used abbreviations and acronyms, as well as executive agencies which have been terminated, transferred or changed names since 1933. Separate indexes are included for personal names and agency or subject.

C. STATE DIRECTORIES

Directory of Staff Assistants to the Governors

Washington, DC: National Governors Association,
1988. Annual.

This work identifies the key staff assistants to governors. The directory is arranged by state and then by function. It is compiled each January for publication in March; users of the directory should consider the possibility that key assistants may change during the course of a year.

Handbook of State Legislative Leaders

Boston, MA: State Legislative Leaders Foundation, 1987. Annual.

Arranged by state, this looseleaf resource provides information on the legislative leadership, including photographs and brief biographies. Chairpersons for legislative committees are identified. Brief narrative information is also provided on campaign finance, lobbying and public access to meetings.

National Directory of State Agencies

9th ed. Bethesda, MD: National Standards Association, Inc., 1988.

The main body of this directory is arranged alphabetically by state and identifies and provides addresses and telephone numbers for the major policy makers of state agencies by functions, such as "aging", "budget", "housing", "taxation and revenue" and "water resources", among others. Another major section arranges the same information provided in the main body by state agency function so that a user may find, for example, all primary policy makers responsible for "economic opportunity." A useful section lists associations of state government officials by state agency function. Therefore, the reader may find, under "budget," the National Association of State Budget Officials, and learn how to contact the association.

State Administrative Officials Classified by Function 1987-88

Lexington, KY: The Council on State Governments, 1987. Biennial.

The third volume in a biennial series which lists the names and addresses of officials in 135 functional areas of state administrative services. Examples of functional areas include "Arts Council", "Energy Resources", "Lottery", "State Fair." Public administrators will find this tool valuable in identifying contact people on the state level in a specific functional area, or in identifying their own counterparts in other states.

State Elective Officials and the Legislatures 1987-1988

Lexington, KY: The Council on State Governments, 1987. Biennial.

Identifies by state the elected executive members and members of the legislature. It also identifies the judges of the highest state court. Home addresses and district numbers along with party affiliation are provided for all members of the legislature.

State Legislative Leadership, Committees & Staff 1987-88

Lexington, KY: The Council on State Governments, 1987. Biennial.

Identifies legislative officers (such as Speaker of the House, majority and minority leaders, etc.) and staff services (such as House Clerk) for each state. Also identifies all standing and joint legislative committees and chairpersons. Legislative agencies are also listed. Addresses and telephone numbers are included. Appendices include selected officers and their addresses for the Senate and the House. There are several appendices identifying selected committees arranged by Committee subject area such as "Agriculture" and then by state, listing the committee Chairperson. Other appendices identify Legislative Reference Libraries and Legislative Service Agencies, both arranged by state.

D. LOCAL DIRECTORIES

County Executive Directory

Washington, DC: Carroll Publishing Company. Semi-annual.

Provides information concerning county government officials. For those counties with at least 25,000 people the entries, arranged by state and then by county, list the county seat, population, provides a phone number for personnel locator services, identifies the major departments and provides the name, phone number and address for the departmental managers. Less complete information is provided for counties of less than 25,000 residents. Also published in a combined edition, *Municipal/County Executive Directory*.

Directory of City Policy Officials

Washington, DC: National League of Cities, 1986. Annual.

A guide identifying municipal executive officials. Cities and towns belonging to the National League of Cities as well as those whose population exceeds 30,000 are arranged alphabetically by state. Each entry lists the form of government, address and telephone number for city hall, title and name of the chief elected official, title and name of the city or town manager, title and name of the presiding officer of the governing body, names of the members of the governing body, and the title and name of the chief administrative officer.

Municipal Executive Directory

Washington, DC: Carroll Publishing Company. Semi-annual.

This directory identifies municipal officials for local governments with populations of at least 15,000. Entries

include population, county and identifies major departments and their managers, providing addresses and telephone numbers. Less complete information is provided for
municipalities of under 15,000 residents.

Municipal Year Book 1989

*Washington, DC: International City Management
Association (ICMA), 1989. Annual.*

An authoritative and indispensable annual source
book on municipal data and development. In most years,
the fifth chapter includes the directories of officials in local
government. Numerous directories are included: state
municipal leagues; state agencies for community affairs;
state municipal management associations; state associations of counties; directors of councils of government;
selected county officials; and elected municipal officials.
An annotated directory of professional, special assistance
and educational organizations serving local and state
governments is included in this chapter. The directory
information is also published by ICMA in a separate
volume. Municipal leagues are identified in this publication.

II. GUIDES TO ACTIVITIES

These sources will provide users with information on the legislative activity of elected officials, especially members of Congress. The section is included because it is important to know what is happening in Washington and how (and which) members of Congress are initiating, supporting or opposing specific legislation.

A. CURRENT ACTIVITIES

Congressional Index

Chicago, IL: Commerce Clearing House (CCH). Biennial with weekly updates.

A two volume looseleaf service which provides current information on each session of Congress. Updated every two weeks, information includes addresses and biographical information on each Senator and Representative, members of each standing and subcommittee, dates of committee meetings and issues discussed, abstracts of all bills filed, their history and current status, resolutions, and each member's vote on each bill considered by the chamber. Separate sections are included for reorganization plans, treaties and nominations. Another section lists enactments and amendments and vetoes. Indexes to facilitate access include subjects, authors, statute citation and names of laws amended or enacted.

Congressional Quarterly Almanac

Washington, DC: Congressional Quarterly, Inc. (CQ). Annual.

One of the most useful reference tools which details the activities of a session of a Congress. It is based upon the *Congressional Quarterly Weekly Report* which details the political activities and the major news events affecting the American political scene. Many of the articles are long and detailed and weekly topical articles are common. Numerous graphs, tables and charts are included. In many instances, the President's news conferences or statements are reprinted in their entirety. Budget status reports are provided as necessary; and each issue includes details on roll-call votes if any occurred. An indispensable source of current information on the happenings in Washington.

The annual is a cumulation of the weekly periodical. Usually beginning with a general background of the Congress including its members and identifying the major events, the almanac is then divided into chapters which parallel the various federal departments. Appendices discuss Supreme Court decisions, elections results and commentary, studies on several key votes, selected presidential messages, brief annotations of all laws passed and roll-call charts. There is a subject-arranged roll-call index and a general index with personal names and subjects.

Current Events Transcripts Service: Guide to Statements and Interviews of Leading Public Figures

Bethesda, MD: Congressional Information Service (CIS), 1988.

This is a weekly index with cumulations to a companion microfiche set of full text of the statements indexed. The microfiche set provides unedited transcripts of all public remarks from the President, major public statements and briefings from other administration officials, as well as speeches at public affairs and public interest news conferences, TV broadcast interviews, speeches by private individuals and other material such as hearings presentations selected from *CIS US Congressional Hearings Index*. This new service greatly improves access to public statements, as any user of *Vital Speeches of the Day* will recognize.

B. GENERAL AND HISTORICAL ACTIVITIES

Congress and the Nation

Volume VI 1981-1984. Washington, DC: Congressional Quarterly, Inc., 1985.

This series begun in 1965; it contains articles detailing congressional activities during a specific years. The first volume is inclusive from 1945 to 1964. Essentially this resource is a cumulation of the articles from each annual *Congressional Quarterly Almanac* for the time period covered by the volume. The articles are arranged chronologically by subject area which generally falls along the lines of federal executive departments. Most of the articles deal with congressional policy decisions and actions. Appendixes include key votes, congressional membership lists, congressional committees, legislative veto opinions, presidential vetoes and presidential texts, as well as political statistical charts. There is a combined subject, title and personal name index.

Congressional Quarterly's Guide to Congress

3rd ed. Washington, DC: Congressional Quarterly, Inc., 1982.

This third edition updates the lengthy articles explaining how Congress evolved and how it works published in the first two editions. All articles include a selected bibliography of resources which will provide more in-depth information. Appendixes include pre-Constitutional documents, congressional statistics back to 1789, rules of the House and the Senate and a glossary of congressional terms. There is a biographical index of members of Congress from 1789 to 1982 and a combined subject, personal name and title index.

Congressional Quarterly, Inc. (CQ) also publishes *Congressional Quarterly's Guide to the Presidency* and *Congressional Quarterly's Guide to the U.S. Supreme Court*, both published in 1989.

State Government: CQ's Guide to Current Issues and Activities 1987-88

Washington, DC: Congressional Quarterly, Inc., 1987. Biennial.

This guide reprints CQ articles discussing state government issues, usually focusing on state-federal relationships. Articles are arranged within eight broad topic areas including elections, parties, polls, state bureaucracies and state issues.

State Policy Reports

A periodical appearing twenty-four times a year from State Policy Research, Inc.

Each issue of this periodical presents information concerning three or four issues related to state government. Many of the articles are summaries and discussions of recent publications or reports. A sampling of reports includes: "State and Local Pension Plans"; "Teacher Salaries and Teacher Shortages"; and "Welfare Prevention". An annual subject index to the articles is available and necessary since *State Policy Reports* is not covered by the indexing services.

III. DIRECTORIES OF THOSE INFLUENCING GOVERNMENT

People other than elected officials and government workers can provide valuable assistance to the public administrator. Several sources are included identifying services which are provided by individuals, or are people-oriented. In addition, the citations list the major resource tool for locating associations, their staff and membership. This list of sources is limited and, since many of these directories are not new publications, users should be aware of how rapidly personnel changes take place in and about Washington, DC.

A. CONSULTANTS

Consultants and Consulting Organizations Directory

8th ed. Detroit, MI: Gale Research Company, 1988.

A two volume set with descriptions of over 10,000 consulting firms and individuals in volume one and the necessary indexes to access the directory in volume two. The directory in volume one is divided into fourteen general subject areas and is then arranged alphabetically by the name of the firm. Each entry includes an address, phone number, identifies the principals and briefly describes the purpose and activity of the firm. Some entries identify recent publications of the principals and those conferences and special services offered by the firm. Indexes in the second volume include: geographic; subject; industries served; personal name; and consulting firms.

Directory of Organizations and Individuals Professionally Engaged in Government Research and Related Activities

Detroit, MI: Governmental Research Association, Inc., 1987. Biennial.

This publication, know also as the *GRA Directory* and *Governmental Research Association Directory*, provides the addresses and phone numbers for local organizations including: governmental research agencies; taxpayers associations; citizen and voter leagues; leagues of municipalities; legislative research agencies and others. Over one hundred national agencies and their addresses are also included in a separate section.

Dun's Consultants Directory 1989

Parsippany, NJ: Dun & Bradstreet, 1989. Annual.

This provides directory information on over 25,000 consulting firms and, as well as the usual directory information, includes annual revenue, number of employees, year started and officers. The main entries are arranged alphabetically by firms; abbreviated entries are arranged by state and city, by specialty and by branch offices geographically.

Minority Consultants and Minority-Owned Consulting Organizations 1988-1989

Charlotte, NC: Atlantic Coast Publishing. Annual.

A listing of minority consultants in business, technical fields, education and training, architecture and design and other fields.

Research Services Directory

3rd ed. Detroit, MI: Gale Research Company, 1987.

A useful guide to private fee-based and contract

research firms and individuals. See also *Online Database Search Services Directory* (1988) in Part 5 of this Desk Book.

B. LOBBYISTS AND LEGAL COUNSEL

Law and Business Directory of Corporate Counsel 1988-89

New York: Prentice Hall, 1988.

As well as corporate legal counsel, this directory includes counsel to not-for-profit organizations, public utilities, port authorities and other semi-governmental bodies. There are separate geographical, firm and individual names indexes.

Martindale-Hubbell Law Directory

121st ed. Summit, NJ: Martindale-Hubbell, Inc., 1989.

This eight volume set is a comprehensive directory of law firms and lawyers in the United States. It also includes the judges in all court systems.

National Directory of Corporate Public Affairs

Washington, DC: Columbia Books, Inc., 1983.

This is a directory of the major corporate Political Action Committees (PAC's). The main entry, by committee, includes addresses, officers, funds received and spent for the previous fiscal year. Half the directory is an alphabetic listing of the leading personnel in the corporate public affairs profession with their position, firm, address and phone number.

Training and Development Organizations Directory

4th ed. Detroit, MI: Gale Research Company, 1988.

This directory includes information on firms, institutes, specialized university programs and other agencies which offer training and development programs. It is intended to assist those seeking information about training opportunities and the organizations that make them available. The directory section is arranged alphabetically by state, then by municipality and then by the organization providing the training. Each entry includes an address and identifies the principal, area of special course emphasis and typical clients and audience; it also includes a brief description of some of the programs offered including their cost.

Washington Lobbyists & Lawyers Directory

6th ed. Washington, DC: Communications Services, 1984.

This is the most recent edition we have seen of a directory to about 10,000 individuals half of whom are registered under the Lobby Registration Act of 1946 or registered as foreign agents. The remainder are Washington legal counsel for various groups and interests. There is an alphabetic name index followed by full information on institution, association, firm or country supporting the individuals.

Washington Representatives

13th ed. Washington, DC: Columbia Books, Inc., 1989. Annual.

A directory of "who does what for whom" in Washington. The directory is arranged alphabetically by the firm or personal name of the representative or lobbyist. Many of the listings of firms provide a list of their clients and identifies the members representing the firms and their backgrounds. There is also a section which provides similar information for organizations that maintain a

Washington office or have representatives in the capitol to represent their interests. An index by broad subject areas lists organizations and representatives likely to be most active in that field of interest.

C. OTHERS

This section includes important directories to federally funded or coordinated programs, projects and research centers. It also includes the principal directories, found in most libraries, for locating officials and membership of the numerous associations and groups, including volunteer service organizations, which seek to influence and supply information to government at various levels.

Community Resources Directory

2nd ed. Detroit, MI: Gale Research Company, 1984.

Public administrators could utilize this directory to locate volunteer programs in their area, training programs for existing or planned volunteer efforts, or to get an idea of how volunteerism is applied throughout the United States as a component in providing services and programs. Entries, whose content varies from section to section, includes adequate information to contact the program or to get an understanding of its efforts. An organization name index and a program emphasis index facilitates use of the directory.

Directories in Print

7th ed. Detroit, MI: Gale Research Company, 1990.

This work provides citations to guides and directories of all types. This is the tool to use for identifying the many published membership directories. The citations are arranged alphabetically within sixteen subject areas by the title of the directory. Each citation gives title, publisher and address, an indication of the directory's coverage, editors and price.

Encyclopedia of Associations 1990

24nd ed. Detroit, MI: Gale Research Company, 1989.

A multiple volume directory with information on over 25,000 associations. This is a valuable resource for public administrators needing to identify associations in specific fields. The directory component titled *Regional, State, and Local Organizations* may be of special interest. Information in each entry includes: address and phone number; when founded; members; staff size; operating budget; description of the association; and when the next convention will be held and where. As with many of Gale's multi-volume directories, we suggest the index volume always be the first one to consult.

Encyclopedia of Associations: Regional, State, and Local Organizations, 1988-89

Detroit, MI: Gale Research Company, 1987. Annual.

Information on nonprofit membership organizations with interstate, state, intrastate, city or local scope, membership and interests. National associations are not included in this component of the Gale set. Entries include an address, operational information and purpose for each identified organization. Each volume includes an alphabetical index to organizational names and keywords.

Government Programs and Projects Directory

Detroit, MI: Gale Research Company, 1983-4.

This three volume set may serve as a starting place when attempting to identify federal departments and agencies administering assistance, research and other types of programs. This publication is not exclusively about grant programs; and although the *Catalog of Federal Domestic Assistance* from the Government Printing Office (GPO) is often cited as a source of information, it in no manner replaces the Catalog. Information for each numbered entry includes the name of the department or agency, address, name of the program, legislative authorization (if known), description of the program, funding levels and source of the information. The work is arranged alphabetically by federal department and then by agency within the department. However, all three volumes include the same federal departments. Therefore, to find all of the programs of the Department of Education will require use of all three volumes. Fortunately, the indexes refer to entries in all volumes.

Government Research Centers Directory

2nd ed. Detroit, MI: Gale Research Company, 1982.

This directory is a descriptive inventory of 1,642 federally administered or substantially supported or federally coordinated research programs. The main text of the directory is arranged alphabetically by name of the research program. Each entry includes the address and telephone number, date established, name of the chief administrator, the federal government reporting unit, the name of the non-federal contractor, university or organization, staffing, type of research activity, publications, library or special collections and other comments which may be useful to the reader. There are three indexes: names and keywords, agency and geographic.

National Trade and Professional Associations of the United States

24th ed. Washington, DC: Columbia Books, Inc., 1989. Annual.

This is an inexpensive directory of over six thousand trade associations, labor unions and professional and other non-profit voluntary associations. The citations are as adequate as those in the *Encyclopedia of Associations* (which, however, lists twenty-five thousand national associations) and there are subject, geographic, budget and executive indexes.

Direct Mail Lists Rates and Data

A periodical service published six times a year by Standard Rate and Data Service.

This business tool is included here because it identifies the many commercial sources of mailing lists. Duns Marketing Service lists, and many other sources, are described in detail in this suppliers and services directory. Mailing list generation is very labor intensive and public administrators should realize that they can purchase custom tailored lists of almost any description quite inexpensively. Consult this directory in a large university library or business library rather than attempting to purchase a copy.

Part 2
STATISTICS

Statistics are used in public administration as a component in a decision making process, for justification in determining a position or developing a policy and for policy evaluation. This chapter will help the student, researcher and practitioner identify some of the major sources of statistics and information about the statistics. There are so many sources of statistics published, produced on microfilm or available in machine-readable form, and so many guides to those statistical sources, that it would require more than a single volume to list them. In fact, to completely indicate the regular statistical series published by the federal government requires more than a single volume. Therefore, this is largely a guide to guides to sources of statistics.

I. GUIDES TO STATISTICAL SOURCES

This section includes resources which identify who gathers, compiles, analyzes and publishes statistics in specific subject areas.

A. DIRECTORIES

These are guides which do not include the statistics themselves, but identify sources which include statistics.

Census Catalog and Guide

Washington, DC: U.S. Bureau of the Census, 1988. Annual.

An annual directory of statistics and other publications available from the Bureau of the Census. Abstracts of publications and statistical series and programs are provided for each entry, arranged within broad subject areas. This is an indispensable source when trying to navigate the thousands of census reports and publications available.

Of special note is an appendix which identifies sources of assistance for information seekers. Organized by service provided and then by state, information is included on state data centers, federal depository libraries and other federal sources of statistics. This appendix will prove valuable to public administrators trying to track down statistical data and other information within, and sometimes about, a state.

Economics Sourcebook of Government Statistics

Lexington, MA: DC Heath and Company, 1983.

This tool identifies economic statistics generated by agencies of the federal government. Each entry identifies the issuing agency and provides descriptive information on the coverage of the statistical data, source of the data, when the series started and limitations of the statistics. Users are also referred to other informational sources and provided with an address and telephone number of the source agency.

Factfinder for the Nation

U.S. Bureau of the Census. Irregular.

These topical brochures describe the census material available on a given subject. Some of the topics covered include manufacturing data, census geography, use of census records, retail trade, population, housing, construction, data for small communities and others. A most useful *Factfinder* describes Census Bureau programs and products (*Factfinder*, Issue #18). Single issues are revised irregularly and are free upon request from the Census Bureau's Customer Services.

Federal Statistical Directory: The Guide to Personnel and Data Sources

28th Edition. Phoenix, AZ: Oryx Press, 1987.

An easy to use resource for identifying sources of statistical information and key contact people. It identifies over 4,000 people in the Executive Office and its various Departments and independent agencies with responsibilities for statistical compilation, organization and analysis. Addresses, titles and telephone numbers are provided. There also is an annotated listing of general sources of federal statistical information and another appendix which identifies, by state, the person and agency designated as a State Data Center by the U.S. Bureau of the Census.

Guide to Statistical Materials Produced by Governments and Associations in the United States

Alexandria, VA: Chadwyck-Healey Inc., 1987.

This guide to statistical sources emphasizes regularly published items and is divided into three sections: national associations, the federal government and the states. Each citation is annotated and identifies the source of data used in the statistical tool which is being cited. The alphabetical arrangement is easy to use. There are separate title and subject indexes. Addresses are provided for those associations and governmental entities identified as a statistical source. State statistics do not include municipal or county sources.

Guide to U.S. Government Statistics

McLean, VA: Documents Index, Inc., 1988. Annual.

This publication is an annotated guide to nearly 12,600 statistical publications of the federal government. The main section is arranged by the Superintendent of Documents classification scheme, which more or less follows an alphabetical organization of the various departments of the Executive Branch. Citations are arranged by the title of the publication. In some cases the entry includes a narrative description of the statistical source. Most entries include an indication of frequency of the publication and when it began.

Handbook of United States Economic and Financial Indicators

Westport, CT: Greenwood Press, 1985.

Identifies and provides descriptions of more than 200 economic and financial measures. Arranged alphabetically, each measure's entry includes a description, derivation, use, publisher, publication title and frequency.

Bibliographic citations are provided for more in-depth information. Indicators are cross referenced and indexed.

Major Programs: Bureau of Labor Statistics

Washington, DC: U.S. Bureau of Labor Statistics, 1985.

A guide to the Bureau's major statistical programs, the data available, coverage, the form of publication, some of the uses of the data and to selected publications and data tapes. The guide includes employment and unemployment statistics, prices and living conditions, wages and industrial relationships, productivity and technology, occupational safety and health statistics and economic growth and employment projections.

Statistics Sources

11th ed. Detroit, MI: Gale Research Company, 1988.

The eleventh edition is a major overhaul of the past editions and is an important reference work. This two volume set provides nearly 60,000 citations to sources of statistical information from around the world. This work will be useful to public administrators in two ways. First, the introductory section includes an annotated bibliography of major governmental and non-governmental statistical sources. Secondly, the sources are arranged alphabetically by subject area. Therefore, if you wish to find statistics on computer use, you only have to look under "Computer" to find two statistical reports on computer use in public schools.

B. INDEXES AND ABSTRACTS

The two following resources provide detailed subject indexing to statistics from original sources and also provide the user with an indicative abstract including the bibliographic information necessary to locate the original source. The subject indexes provide code numbers which are the key to both the indicative abstracts and to microfiche sets of the full documents.

American Statistical Index

Bethesda, MD: Congressional Information Service. Annual with monthly supplements.

A comprehensive guide and index to the statistical publications of the U.S. Government published in two parts: the Index and the Abstracts. The Index is published monthly, cumulated quarterly and then cumulated annually into a single volume. It is available online, as *ASI*, from Dialog. Its primary arrangement is by subject and name. These are cross referenced as appropriate to other subject headings. The Index citations give the title of the report or document, its type and a code or key number that directs the reader to a volume and document number in the separately published Abstracts.

The Abstracts are published monthly and cumulated into a single volume annually. Each Abstract identifies the publisher of the statistics, the title of the report, a summary of the reports contents and may indicate the statistical information (such as tables) provided by or in the report or document. Arrangement of each volume is by executive department (not in alphabetical order, so the browser must use the table of contents to locate the department) and then by the four digit agency identification number. Abstract descriptions are more than adequate to provide the reader with an idea of what is included in the agency's publication.

It is most useful to conduct the inquiry first in the Index, retrieve the necessary code numbers, and then refer to the Abstracts. Information is also included in each issue and with the Abstracts on how to obtain a copy of the source document. Congressional Information Service sells the corresponding statistical documents in a microfiche set.

Congressional Information Service has announced a CD-ROM which will provide for efficient computer terminal search of both this and the following database.

Statistical Reference Index

Bethesda, MD: Congressional Information Service, Inc. Annual with monthly supplements.

This is the most complete source of indexing and abstracting of American statistical publications from sources other than the U.S. Government. There are two parts: the Index and the Abstracts. The Index is published monthly (except for the combined January-February issue), cumulated quarterly and then cumulated annually. Thus far, there is one five year cumulation. The main arrangement of the tool is by subject and names. Coverage excludes: highly localized data; scientific and highly technical data; publications with limited or exclusive distribution; publications which simply republish federal data from a single source without analysis; and most importantly, publications of municipal and county data. The citation in the Index provides a title of the statistical source and the type of publication it is, such as an annual report.

Abstracts are produced monthly, cumulated annually and key to the alphanumeric code number of the Index. Because of the manner in which the Index cumulates, it is much easier to use the Index to locate a citation to an Abstract rather than use the Abstracts without the Index. The Abstracts are arranged by issuing source: Associations, Business Organizations, Commercial Publishers, Independent Research Organizations, State Governments and Universities. Abstract citations are fairly complete and identify the statistical publisher, provide information about the publication and includes other useful descriptions of the publication especially related to statistical charts and tables. The code number also gives access to the microfiche set of the majority of documents, those which CIS has received permission to reproduce.

C. STATISTICAL POLICY

The following handbooks give the statistical policies of the federal government. These policies determine the statistical gathering, analysis and disseminating process.

Federal Statistical System 1980 to 1985

Washington, DC: Congressional Research Service of the Library of Congress, 1985.

An Update of the Status of Major Federal Statistical Agencies Fiscal Year 1986

Washington, DC: Congressional Research Service of the Library of Congress, 1987.

The main volume examines the status of the Federal statistical system by department, especially in identifying financial resources and discussing issues. It describes the changes in federal statistical budgets and programs since FY1980 and it reviews the role of the Office of Management and Budget in executing the statistical policy and coordination provisions of the Paperwork Reduction Act of 1980.

The update volume is an analysis of the effects of the administration's proposed FY1986 budget on the programs and policies of eight major federal statistical agencies.

Statistical Policy Handbook

Washington, DC: U.S. Office of Federal Statistical Policy and Standards, 1978.

This handbook provides a convenient source of Federal Statistical Directives and information about interagency committees which have a significant role in compiling and generating federal statistics. The Directives establish uniform statistical standards and guidelines for the collection and compilation of statistical data and for the release and publication of federal statistics.

D. STATISTICS ANNOUNCEMENT PERIODICALS

The major statistical periodicals are described in section IV of this part of the *Desk Book* and in Part 4. They are also indexed through the SUBJECT INDEX. Two current awareness publications of the Census Bureau are described here.

Census and You

Monthly from the U.S. Bureau of the Census.

An informal newsletter published to inform about surveys, products and reports issued by the Bureau of the Census. Short articles highlight statistical information recently compiled.

Monthly Products Announcement

Monthly from the U.S. Bureau of the Census.

This is a listing of all Bureau products issued for a month including reports, computer tapes and disks, maps and microfiche. Organized by publications and data files, the citations include title, series and price. It is free upon request by contacting the Census Bureau's Customer Services.

E. GUIDES TO ONLINE STATISTICAL DATABASES AND SERVICES

There are statistical databases of all types available from the federal government. The following are directories which will identify these and indicate how to access them. See Part 5, ONLINE SERVICES, of this *Desk Book* for the government's non-statistical databases and for services which make value-added presentations online of government statistics.

Directory of Computer Software

Washington, DC: National Technical Information Service, 1987. Annual.

This volume provides abstracts of 1,700 computer programs compiled in cooperation with more than 100 Federal agencies. Arranged by subject areas, entries describe the software and its functions, technical needs and availability. Statistical programs predominate and a subject index facilitates access.

Directory of Computerized Data Files

Washington, DC: National Technical Information Service, 1987.

Provides current information on the availability and content of federal machine-readable data files which are available from the National Technical Information Service. Abstracts of more than 1,200 data files from fifty federal agencies are arranged within broad subject areas including economics, social studies and science and technology. Entries include a description of the data file, keywords in the data file and availability. Indexes are included for subject and agency.

Federal Database Finder

2nd ed. Chevy Chase, MD: Information USA, Inc., 1987.

A directory of some 4,200 free and fee-based databases and files available from the federal government. Entries are arranged alphabetically by name of the database or the federal department and lists a contact person, address and briefly describes the database.

Federal Statistical Data Bases: A Comprehensive Catalog of Current Machine-Readable and Online Files

Phoenix, AZ: Oryx Press, 1988.

This is the successor to the 1981 *Directory of Federal Statistical Data Files* first published by the U.S. Department of Commerce. It is a guide for helping users of federal data bases locate information made available in machine-readable form. It includes nearly 2,500 abstracts describing statistical and related data files, focusing primarily on statistical information on computer tape. Statistical information on disks and online are also covered.

The guide is arranged by federal executive department, and their agencies. It includes independent agencies, boards, committees and commissions. Entries provide data base title, content description, technical description and availability. The work is indexed by subject.

II. GENERAL STATISTICS SOURCES

This section of the *Desk Book* selects statistics sources which are general in nature and broad in coverage.

Almanac of the 50 States

Palo Alto, CA: Information Publications, 1989. Annual.

Most of the information in this annual work is compiled from federal government publications and duplicates information available in other sources. However, by compiling statistical information in one place the almanac serves a purpose in being an easily used reference tool. There is a statistical and informational profile of each state including: state summary; geography and environment; demographics and characteristics of the population; vital statistics and health; education; social insurance and welfare programs; housing and construction; government and elections; governmental finance; crime, law enforcement and courts; labor and income; economy, business, industry and agriculture; and communication, energy and transportation. A profile for the United States as a whole is also included. Following the profiles are more than fifty tables of comparative statistical rankings by state.

Book of the States

Lexington, KY: The Council of State Governments, 1988-89. Biennial.

An important reference tool containing state data and information. There are ten chapters on the states: Constitutions; Executive Branch; Legislative Branch; Judicial Branch; Elections; Finances; Management and Administration; Selected Activities, Issues and Services; Intergovernmental Affairs; and statistics and information.

There is an effort to balance the data tables and statistics with meaningful subject articles. Although this tool is more than just hundreds of tables bound together between two covers, the detail and subject scope of the comparative state tables and charts is the major feature. There is no other reference tool which provides in one place the same topic coverage and depth as this publication. Original sources of information are indicated on the tables.

Historical Statistics of the United States, Colonial Times to 1970

Washington, DC: U.S. Bureau of the Census, 1975.

A two volume set of some 12,500 time series statistics from 1789 forward. Areas covered by the statistics include, but are not limited to, population, labor, prices, natural resources, industry, finances and government. Essential reference for anyone needing time-series statistics prior to 1970.

1980 Census of Population

Washington, DC: U.S. Bureau of the Census.

Every ten years, on the 0 year, the United States takes a snapshot of itself on April 1. The result is a compilation of statistics on a wide range of characteristics of the population and its activities. In the period just before April 1, 1990, the Census Bureau expects to count and describe 250 million people and 106 million housing units. Here is a description of the major reports of the 1980 census:

Census of Population and Housing

Provides statistical data on population such as race, ancestry, occupation, income and on housing such as occupancy, utilization, structural, equipment and financial and household characteristics of housing units for states and census tracts in metropolitan statistical areas.

Detailed Population Characteristics

Includes citizenship, languages spoken at home, residence in 1975, education, marital status, household information, labor force, occupation, income and poverty for the United States, geographic regional areas and standard consolidated statistical areas.

General Social and Economic Characteristics

This is probably the most widely used volume and appears in a United States summary and by states and includes race, birth place, education, occupation, income, language, mobility and many other details.

Congressional District Data Book of the 98th Congress

Provides some of the above data organized by each state's congressional districts.

State Policy Data Book

Alexandria, VA: State Policy Research, Inc., 1988. Annual.

This is a looseleaf notebook with over 400 tables of comparative statistical data from the fifty states on demographics, economics, finances, taxes, spending and employment, federal impacts, education, welfare and social services, health, crime and law enforcement, transportation, natural resources, science and technology, labor, management and local government. Each table includes a numeric value indicating a state's ranking for the statistic covered by each table. A section, "Notes to Tables & Maps," gives the source of the data for each table. A brief index of about 135 subjects provides references to the tables included in the various sections.

Statistical Abstract of the United States 1989

109th edition. Washington, DC: U.S. Bureau of the Census, 1989. Annual.

The *Statistical Abstract* has been published annually since 1878 and is the standard summary of statistics on the social, political and economic organization of the United States. Its hundreds of tables are distributed through more than thirty sections divided by subject areas such as vital statistics, elections and manufacturers. A detailed subject index facilitates access to the data.

There are several important appendixes. Appendix I is a listing of national, state and foreign sources used to compile the statistics. The national sources are listed by subject areas which is very useful to the reader searching for other statistical works. Appendix III lists the principle statistical sources used in several of the sections and discusses their statistical methodology and reliability.

County and City Data Book 1988

Washington, DC: Department of Commerce, Bureau of the Census, 1988.

These are statistics compiled by federal agencies and departments arranged by counties, cities and towns with 25,000 or more inhabitants and places with 2,500 or more inhabitants, presented alphabetically by state within the statistical subject area. It is published as a supplement to the *Statistical Abstract*.

State and Metropolitan Area Data Book 1986

Washington, DC: Department of Commerce, U.S. Bureau of the Census, 1986.

These are statistics compiled by the federal government arranged by subject for geographic areas which include metropolitan areas and components, central cities of metropolitan statistical areas and regions (such as northeast and north central), divisions (such as New England, Middle Atlantic) and the states.

III. FINANCE AND GOVERNMENT OPERATIONS STATISTICS

For the public administration practitioner, student or researcher, statistical information on governmental activities such as finance or governmental operations is always a necessity. The following notes describe some of the statistical sources available on governmental activities and works providing governmental budget statistics and explanation of the accounting and auditing of governmental financial data.

A. FINANCIAL STATISTICS

Annual Survey of Government Finances

Washington, DC: U.S. Bureau of the Census. Annual.

The U.S. Bureau of the Census conducts annual surveys covering the entire range of government finance activities (revenue, expenditure, debt and assets). The most recent was published in 1988 for 1986-87. This *Government Finances* series includes the following reports:

City Government Finances

Provides statistical data on revenues and expenditures for selected cities and urban towns and townships of populations exceeding 50,000. Data is provided for certain municipal services such as education and police and there is information on debt. Separate tables with financial statistics are provided for cities exceeding 300,000 populations.

County Government Finances

Provides statistical financial data including revenues, expenditures, debt, cash and security holdings, utilities, liquor stores and employee retirement systems for county government. Several tables provide more detail for counties with populations exceeding 100,000 and 500,000.

Governmental Finances

Serves as the comprehensive summary of the annual survey findings. Statistical tables are provided for revenues, expenditures, capital outlay, debt and cash and security holdings, utilities, employee retirement systems and insurance trusts for federal, state and local levels of government. Other tables are included on population and personal income and relational statistics and rankings for state and local governments based upon per capita levels.

Local Government Finances in Major County Areas

Provides county government finance data for counties exceeding 100,000 in population. Data is included on revenues, expenditures, debt outstanding and cash and security holdings of local governments by county area.

State Government Finances

Provides statistical financial information on states including finances, expenditures, revenues, debt and cash and security holdings, liquor stores and utilities, insurance trusts, per capita and per $1,000 personal income tables, among other indicators.

State Government Tax Collections

Provides financial statistical data on state revenues by type of tax, sales and gross receipts, license taxes, excise taxes and other sources of revenue. It also includes summary and ranking tables.

Census of Governments

Washington, DC: U.S. Bureau of the Census.

Every five years since 1957, on years ending with 2 and 7, a census is completed on U.S. government finance. The 1982 *Census of Governments* was issued in 1985. Titles in the series include:

Government Organization

Contains the official count of the number of state and local governments and tabulations by type of government and state and county location.

Taxable Property Values and Assessment - Sales Price Ratios

Government Employment

Includes the reports on employment of major local government, a compendium of public employment and information on labor-management relationships in state and local governments.

Governmental Finances

This multi-volume set includes:

- **Finances of Public School Systems**
- **Finances of Special Districts**
- **Finances of County Government**
- **Finances of Municipal and Township Governments**
- **Compendium of Government Finances**

Local Government in Metropolitan Areas

Topical Studies

This is also a multi-volume set and includes coverage of state and local government employee

retirement systems, state payments to local governments, historical statistics and graph presentation
of statistics from other volumes;

Guide to the Census of Governments

Describes procedures followed in conducting
the census.

Facts and Figures on Government Finance, 1988-89

*24th ed. Washington, DC: Tax Foundation;
Baltimore, MD: Johns Hopkins University Press,
1988. Biennial.*

This is a very handy information service which includes 283 tables of financial data documenting the taxing
and spending activities at federal, state and local levels.
Where appropriate, data includes longitudinal information so that trends can be identified and studied. Sources
of data are explained in an introduction to the tables and
further source information is included with each table. A
glossary of terms with brief annotations is included.

Significant Features of Fiscal Federalism

*1989 edition. Washington, DC: Advisory
Commission on Intergovernmental Relations, 1989.*

An annual publication in two volumes. One volume
includes tables on charts on fiscal trends with state-by-state
longitudinal data since 1929 and federal, state and local tax
rates. Volume II includes tables and charts on the distribution of revenue sources, distribution of expenditures by
function, time-series data and state-local rankings.

B. BUDGET, ACCOUNTING AND AUDITING INFORMATION

Budget of the United States Government; Fiscal Year 1990

Washington, DC: Office of Management and Budget, 1989. Annual.

In addition to the President's budget message and an overview of the annual budget, the six volumes in this set contain detailed information on appropriations and funds, special analyses of program areas, historical tables, budgetary details of major policy initiatives and federal debt, federal receipts and federal expenditure data. One brief volume, *United States Budget in Brief*, presents a nontechnical overview of the budget for the general public. The volume titled *Appendix* is the one that contains detailed information on appropriation and funds. It is the volume that contains the text of appropriation language, the budget schedules and provides the current item estimate along with the two previous actual or estimated amounts.

Economic Report of the President, Together with the Annual Report of the Council of Economic Advisers

Washington, DC: U.S. Government Printing Office, 1988. Annual.

This economic report, submitted each February, is a valuable compilation of information. It includes discussion and data on the performance and prospects of the economy. Statistical tables relating to employment, personal income, production, foreign trade and other issues are presented. These are usually time-series presentations; they are from a variety of governmental and nongovernmental agencies and organizations.

Financing State and Local Governments

4th ed. Washington, DC: Brookings Institute, 1986.

This source examines major state and local taxes and documents trends influencing them. There are chapters describing governmental transfers, state taxes, local taxes, debt, retirement systems, capital budgets and local fiscal performance and capacity. Many tables are included in the text along with an appendix of statistical tables.

Guide to Audits of Local Governments

Fort Worth, TX: Practitioners Publishing Co., 1986. Loose-leaf.

This set is designed to assist local government financial officers in handling audits. It describes governmental accounting standards, auditing standards, audit sampling and various audit programs. Extensive practitioner material is included: guides, checklists, forms for various audit programs, etc.

Moody's Municipal and Government Manual

New York: Moody's Investors Service, Inc. Monthly with annual cumulations.

This is one of several major information services published primarily for investors. We suggest that those pursuing information on municipal and other public finance bonds consult *Public Finance: An Information Sourcebook* described further in APPENDIX B of this *Desk Book*.

Standard & Poor's Bond Guide

New York: Standard & Poor's Corporation. Monthly with microfiche annual.

This tool also covers more than 15,000 corporate, municipal, convertible and industrial revenue bonds. It includes the S&P ratings on nearly 10,000 municipal and toll revenue bonds.

IV. ECONOMIC, BUSINESS AND LABOR STATISTICS

The following citations identify the major, most readily available sources of economic, business and labor statistics. Most are periodical publications of the federal government. Part 5, ONLINE SERVICES, describes the online and machine-readable forms of this data.

Business Conditions Digest

Monthly from the U.S. Bureau of Economic Analysis.

The purpose of this monthly publication is to help businesses and others, such as governments, evaluate business conditions. Part I contains charts and tables of 150 time series; about three-fourths are individual cyclical indicators, the balance are related analytical measures. Cyclical indicators are defined as economic time series which have been singled out as leading, lagging or coincident based upon their conformity to cyclical movements in aggregate economic activity. Part II includes about 140 charts and tables of time series which do not conform well to business cycles but are of value to business analysts and forecasters.

Business Serials of the U.S. Government

2nd ed. Chicago, IL: American Library Association, 1988.

This gives further guidance to business service journals and series publications of the federal government. They are described and subject indexed by this work. The majority are statistical publications.

CPI Detailed Report

Monthly from the U.S. Bureau of Labor Statistics.

This reports consumer price movements, including statistical tables and technical notes. Focus is on the consumer price index which is tabulated by product, commodity and service group, and by region and selected local areas.

Economic Indicators

Monthly from the U.S. Council of Economic Advisors.

Statistical tables and charts of forty-five economic indicators are divided into seven areas: total output, income and spending; employment, unemployment and wages; production and business activity; prices; money, credit and security markets; federal finance; and international statistics. The "Contents" page on the back cover serves as the index.

Federal Reserve Bulletin

Monthly from the Board of Governors of the Federal Reserve System.

Issues include several timely and topical articles, most with statistical charts and tables. Every issue includes current U.S. banking and monetary statistics. They are arranged into sections on domestic financial statistics (banking and finance, real estate and several tables on federal finance), domestic nonfinancial statistics (labor force, industrial production, consumer prices, personal income and savings and others) and international statistics (such as U.S. foreign trade and banks and banking outside the United States). Statistical tables are indexed in each issue. Also see *The Fed in Print* published twice a year from the Federal Reserve Bank of Philadelphia described further in Part 4 of this Desk Book. It indexes the *Federal Reserve Bulletin* and the numberous publications, many of regional interest, from the thirteen Federal Reserve Banks. It also gives the source addresses.

Handbook of Basic Economic Statistics

Monthly from Economic Status Bureau of Washington, DC.

Established in 1947 by a private research organization, the Handbook is a compilation of more than 1,800 statistical series relating to all aspects of the national economy. The data is condensed from the data released by the federal government. Each issue is cumulative and includes comparable annual data back to 1913 or to the first year thereafter for which figures are available. Statistics for the current year and several preceding years are published in full monthly or quarterly detail. There is a subject index.

Handbook of Labor Statistics

Washington, DC: U.S. Bureau of Labor Statistics. Biennial.

This is a publication of statistical tables on all aspects of labor including: employment; unemployment; work experience; educational attainment; hours and earnings by industry; pay; general wage and benefit changes; consumer and producer prices; export and import prices; work stoppage statistics; occupational injuries and illnesses; and foreign labor statistics. Many tables include longevity data and several data elements are divided into geographic regions. Without an index, the primary access is the tables of contents. For data within the last three years, see *Monthly Labor Review*.

Monthly Labor Review

Monthly from the U.S. Bureau of Labor Statistics.

This publication has a section called "Current Labor Statistics" which includes 48 tables on comparative indicators, labor force data, labor compensation and collective bargaining data, price data, productivity data, international comparisons and injury and illness data. Data on longevity is included in the charts and some tables.

Standard & Poor's Statistical Service

New York: Standard & Poor's Corporation.
Loose-leaf with monthly updates.

This is a most useful source of statistical information on: banking and finance; production and labor; price indexes; income and trade; building; electric power and fuels; metals; transportation; textiles, chemicals and paper; agricultural products; and security price index records. The most current statistics are first arranged within the industry areas listed above; then time-series data, often in monthly or quarterly increments, is presented.

Survey of Current Business

Monthly from the U.S. Department of Commerce,
Bureau of Economic Analysis.

This monthly publication is the most important single source for estimates and analyses of U.S. economic activity and current U.S. business statistics. Each issue includes a narrative on the "Business Situation" which contains statistical data. Statistical tables are also provided for selected national income and product accounts and composite indexes of leading, coincident and lagging indicators. Each issue then presents as many as five topical articles with statistical tables. Usually during the course of the calendar year several articles will appear with statistical tables concerning governmental finances and fiscal conditions.

At the end of each issue are blue pages of tables that present over 1,900 major economic series of current business statistics. Often the series statistics include a total from two preceding years and a monthly breakdown for the past fourteen months. These statistical tables update the biennial supplement *Business Statistics* that presents the historical data and the methodological notes for the series that appear in the Survey.

The U.S. Bureau of Economic Analysis also publishes another supplement, *National Income and Products Accounts of the United States.*

U.S. Industrial Outlook

Washington, DC: U.S. International Trade Administration, 1989. Annual.

This presents industry review articles with statistical tables and charts and forecasts. Users need to give attention to the Standard Industrial Classification (SIC) system of identifying industries. These do not always correspond to what we think of as an industry. Additional reference sources and a subject index to the 350 industries discussed, are included.

V. VOTING STATISTICS

This section identifies two statistical sources with information on elections. Other reference tools concerning voting and election statistics are identified in the first section of this part of the *Desk Book*. Additional statistical information on voting in the state and local levels may be found through local newspapers or from the reports of the local and state election officials indexed in *Statistical Reference Index* and *Index to Current Urban Documents*.

America Votes

Volume 17. Washington, DC: Elections Research Center, 1987.

This is a series publication that details voting statistics for presidential primaries and elections and for governors and members of Congress on the state level. Balloting results for Governor by county are also provided.

Congressional Quarterly's Guide to U.S. Elections

2nd ed. Washington, DC: Congressional Quarterly Inc., 1985.

A series of articles about, and results from, political party conventions along with election statistics from presidential, House and Senate and gubernatorial elections dating back to 1789. Appendixes include information on each session of Congress since 1789, political party affiliation of members of each congressional session and immigrant statistics by country and year. Specific indexes include candidates for presidential, gubernatorial, House and the Senate. A general index provides personal name and subject access.

VI. PUBLIC OPINION DATA

A type of statistical information frequently cited in day to day public administration is public opinion poll results. Pollsters are continually asking the American public for their reactions to issues and current events. Many of these polls are commissioned by the media and our primary access to them is temporary, through what we see, read and hear on that day. However, the following are sources of polls or guides to identifying polls. In addition to what is noted here, indexes to newspapers and to weekly news magazines are a good source for locating public opinion statistics. The *Statistical Reference Index* also identifies public opinion poll statistics.

American Public Opinion Index

Louisville, KY: Opinion Research Service. Annual.

This resource indexes some 1600 questions polled by over 140 organizations. The responses to the questions indexed are found in the companion microfiche set *American Public Opinion Data* published by Opinion Research Service. The Index also informs users how to contact the polling organization in order to get the responses.

Gallup Report

Monthly from the Gallup Poll Organization.

Each monthly issue has several issue-oriented polls. Questions are followed by responses in statistical tables.

Guide to Resources and Services

Ann Arbor, MI: Inter- University Consortium for Political and Social Research (ICPRSR). Irregular.

This is an annotated bibliography of the machine-readable data collections of numerous studies held by the ICPSR, a consortium of 260 colleges and universities in sixteen countries. The guide is organized into subject areas and the subject index is most useful in locating a particular study. Many of the data files held by the Consortium include public opinion data.

Public Opinion

Bimonthly from American Enterprise Institute for Public Policy Research.

This journal has publishing information on polls since 1978.

Public Opinion Quarterly

Quarterly from the American Association for Public Opinion Research.

This journal includes articles on public opinion polls and issues. Each issue usually includes the study and the results of at least one public opinion poll.

The Gallup Poll

Wilmington, DE: Scholarly Resources, Inc., 1988. Annual.

Annual volumes have been published since 1978 with a five volume set containing public opinion statistics from 1935 to 1977. Arranged chronologically by date of poll in every year back to 1935, this reference set provides the statistical results of Gallup polls. Each entry provides the interview dates, the methodology used to gather the data (mail or telephone survey, etc.), the question asked and the responses. Responses may be a simple "agree" or "disagree" and then may include the geographic area, income, education, political party, religion, gender, age and other characteristics of the respondents. The subject index at the end of each annual volume is necessary.

Part 3
TERMS, RESEARCH METHODS AND PUBLISHING

This Part identifies and provides brief description of a highly miscellaneous but very important collection of research tools for the public administration practitioner or researcher. Tools dealing with public administration terminology, research methods, libraries and governmental and public interest publishing activity will overlap and reiterate each other quite often. Our method in this *Desk Book* has been to select the most recent tools, and ones we have used or examined, and to provide enough annotation so that you might determine their particular value to you. All the titles here also appear under appropriate subjects in the SUBJECT INDEX at the end of the *Desk Book.*

I. DICTIONARIES AND HANDBOOKS

These dictionaries and handbooks will help the reader discover or clarify definitions of terms and concepts related to public administration.

AMA Management Handbook

2nd ed. New York: American Management Association, 1983.

This is a general management reference tool which public administrators will find useful because of its broad coverage of management terms, issues and functions. Over 200 management experts contributed to the discussion of the subdisciplines of management. Chapters include general management, finance, human resource management, employee benefits and public relations, among others. There is a combined personal name, subject and contributors index.

American Political Dictionary

New York: Holt, Rinehart and Winston, 1982.

This book defines nearly 1,200 terms relating to American governmental institutions, practices and problems. Definitions are cross-referenced to other definitions within the book. Numerous court decisions are also included. An index is provided for all definitions.

Blackwell Encyclopedia of Political Institutions

New York: Basil Blackwell, 1987.

Arranged alphabetically, this work provides lengthy definitions of political institutions. Many of the terms are defined in the context of Europe as well as the United States. Most entries include bibliographic citations to further readings. All definitions are signed and prepared with care. An index to subjects is included.

Encyclopedia of Management

3rd ed. New York: Van Nostrand Reinhold Company, 1982.

An carefully prepared "A to Z" reference handbook on management. Most articles include reference to other information sources including associations, periodicals and textbooks.

Encyclopedia of the American Constitution

New York: Macmillan, 1986.

This is a major encyclopedia, in four volumes, and it can be found in most libraries. With its glossary of legal terms, case index, detailed subject index, appendices and 2,200 articles, it is the first place to look for any inquiry related to constitutional law. It was begun in 1978 and completed for the bicentennial and thus is as current as the Gramm-Rudman-Hollings Balanced Budget Act (1985).

Facts on File Dictionary of Public Administration

New York: Facts on File Publications, 1985.

A dictionary which includes concepts, laws, journals, court cases and organizations. Entries include cross references to other entries and other sources as appropriate. It includes biographical entries to significant figures in the history and current practice of public administration. Laws that directly influence public administration are summarized. The length of entries varies from a few words to several hundred.

Handbook of Human Resources Administration

2nd ed. New York: McGraw-Hill Book Company, 1986.

Although many of the articles are specific to the private sector, the public administrator will find articles relevant to their public sector personnel administration needs, especially because of the practitioner-oriented, nuts and bolts approach of most contributors. Areas discussed include: development of human resources; recruitment, selection and placement; wage and salary administration; employee appraisal and assessment; labor relations; and communicating to employees, among others.

Public Administration Dictionary

2nd ed. New York: John Wiley & Sons, 1988.

Entries are arranged alphabetically within subject oriented chapters. Fundamentals of public administration, public policy, public management, bureaucracy and administrative organization, personnel administration, financial administration and public law and regulation are covered. Most of the definitions are quite long, some up to several hundred words and more, and are cross referenced to other entries. Following each definition is a paragraph discussing the significance of the term to the field of public administration.

Safire's Political Dictionary

New York: Balantine Books, 1980.

William Safire's A-Z dictionary defines about 1,600 terms in 1,200 entries. Cross-references are provided at the end of the definitions when appropriate. Most of the definitions are phrases used in contemporary political discussion and are attributed to the author when possible. Many of the definitions are quite long. Included is a chapter on how the terms were researched, bibliography and a combined subject-name index which includes cross-references.

State and Local Government Political Dictionary

Santa Barbara, CA: ABC-CLIO, 1988.

This describes the major concepts and terms used in the study of American state and local government and provides guidance to some of the major reference tools, associations and methods useful to this study.

II. RESEARCH METHODS

A. GENERAL REFERENCE TOOLS

These sources will help the user find other reference and information sources in many subject areas.

American Reference Books Annual, 1989

Littleton, CO: Libraries Unlimited, 1989. Annual.

This tool reviews English-language reference books. Reviews are arranged within subject areas, and all reviews are signed. Because of the resource's arrangement, readers may quickly identify reference works within their subject areas of interest. There are separate indexes for author and title and for subject.

Bibliographic Index

New York: H.W. Wilson Company. Published three times a year, annual cumulation.

This index is a subject list of bibliographies published separately or appearing as parts of books, pamphlets and periodicals. Many public administration fields and subjects are included in this index's coverage. About 2,600 periodicals are examined regularly. *Bibliographic Index* dates back to 1937; however, it is mainly valuable for providing this kind of special subject index to many current periodicals. Recent year are searchable online from H.W. Wilson Company.

Guide to Reference Books

10th ed. Chicago, IL: American Library Association, 1986.

Edited by Eugene P. Sheehy, and often referred to as *Sheehy*, this is generally known as the standard guide to

reference books by librarians. The directory is an annotated bibliography of reference books in many disciplines.
The indicative annotations are excellent. In many instances the editor has provided a useful, brief introduction to the reference materials in a subject area. A nearly
300 page personal name, title and subject index will assist
the reader in locating materials.

Sources of Information in the Social Sciences, A Guide to the Literature

3rd ed. Chicago, IL: American Library Association, 1986.

An annotated bibliography of sources in the various
disciplines of the social sciences. Arranged by broad
subjects, by types of sources (such as Current Bibliographies) and by narrower subject fields, this resource guide
is a good starting place for public administrators searching for reference and non-reference materials in the social
sciences. Further, there is a chapter of resources in
Political Science which includes resources in public management. The index includes personal names, titles and
subjects.

Where to Find What: A Handbook to Reference Service

Rev. ed. Metuchen, NJ: The Scarecrow Press, Inc., 1984.

Like *Sheehy*, this also provides citations to reference
books, organized by subject. Almost 1,000 subject areas
are covered in this work. Annotations are provided for
each reference source cited.

World Almanac and Book of Facts

New York: Pharos Books.

Published annually since 1868, the *World Almanac*
is a general reference tool which provides brief informa-

tion, usually by lists and charts, on thousands of topics. Often used as a starting place in seeking information, there is usually an indication of the original source of the facts presented.

B. GRANT REFERENCE TOOLS

There are dozens of resources available for grants writing. These citations to selected resources are included to identify the more important resources on grants and to emphasize the importance grants writing may have for the practitioner. Those who need further information may examine the databases, publications and libraries maintained by the Foundation Center, the Taft Corporation and others. See the *Foundation Directory*, below, and library tools described in the next section to locate these.

Annual Register of Grant Support: A Directory of Funding Sources

Wilmette, IL: National Register Publishing Company. Annual.

This directory provides information on nearly 2,700 grant support programs of government agencies, public and private foundations, corporations, community trusts, unions, educational and professional associations and special interest associations. Each entry includes the name of the grant-making organization, address, names of the grant programs, description of the programs, purpose, legal basis, eligibility, financial data, application information or reference for further information, contact person and other related information. The entries appear in alphabetical order in one of eleven major areas and are further subdivided into more specific subject fields. There are four indexes to facilitate searching this comprehensive volume: subject, organization and program, geographical and personnel.

Catalog of Federal Domestic Assistance

Washington, DC: U.S. Government Printing Office.

The "wish book" of federal grant programs. The base volume and the update are most important resources when considering approaching the federal government for assistance because it provides information on the hundreds of grant programs, projects, services and activities which provide assistance or benefits to the American public administered by federal departments and agencies.

The indexes are useful because they help the reader identify the five digit program code associated with each project. Almost any communication with grant making agencies will require referral to the five digit program number from the *Catalog of Federal Domestic Assistance*. Furthermore, the program descriptions in the Catalog are arranged by this coding system. The information included in each program description includes: federal agency; authorization; objectives; uses and use restrictions; eligibility requirements; application and award process; assistance requirements; regulations, guidelines and literature; information contacts, including telephone numbers; examples of funded projects; and criteria for selecting proposals.

Sections include information on how to write a grant and additional sources of information on grants and grant writing. Another section provides the reader with a method of cross checking the assistance programs with the Appendix to the Federal Budget. This information helps the user learn what the Administration's budget plans are for the program.

Federal Register

Washington, DC: U.S. Government Printing Office. Daily.

Published business days, the *Federal Register* is a resource for learning about grant programs administered by Federal agencies. Announcements for grant programs usually appear within the Notices section of the Register. It is searchable online through several online services.

Foundation Directory

11th ed. New York: The Foundation Center, 1987. Annual.

One of the standard tools for locating information concerning non-governmental sources of grant funds. All foundations included in the Directory held assets of at least one million dollars and provided funding for the last year of record of at least $100,000. Information is based upon IRS returns. The directory section is arranged alphabetically by state and then by foundation. Information for each entry includes address, financial data, purpose and activities, types of support, limitations, application information, officers and their federal employer identification number. Several indexes facilitate access to the foundations: donors, officers and trustees; geographic; types of support; subject; and foundation name. It is available online through Dialog as *FOUNDATION DIRECTORY* and the online *NATIONAL FOUNDATIONS* provides less detailed information of all private U.S. foundations, regardless of size.

A useful section of the print directory lists the publications of The Foundation Center while another lists members of The Foundation Center Network maintaining collections of materials useful for those seeking information on foundation funding and other grant information.

The Foundation Grants Index

16th ed. New York: The Foundation Center, 1987. Annual.

This is a listing of grants of at least $5,000 made by the largest one hundred foundations in the United States. The Index is arranged alphabetically by state and then by foundation name. Each entry provides information on each award including recipient, grant amount, date, purpose and source of information. The intention of the Index is to enable grant seekers to identify the current interests of these foundations and to provide an initial list of potential funding sources. The online database, *FOUNDA-TION GRANTS INDEX* through Dialog, makes use of the data much easier. Readers will need to use other reference sources, such as *The Foundation Directory*, to find more detailed information about the foundations themselves.

Guide to Grants: Governmental and Nongovernmental

2nd ed. Newton, MA: Government Research Publications, 1985.

This is a how-to resource on grants writing, divided into six parts, prepared by Donald Levitan. The first is a series of chapters which describe the grants process. Sources of information on government and nongovernment grants is the second part, with helpful assistance on how to use the *Catalog of Federal Domestic Assistance* and other federal information sources and a list with addresses of the top fifty grant making foundations. Part three discusses the various components of the grant application and the remaining parts provide a bibliography, checklists and a discussion of grants management.

C. LIBRARY RESEARCH TOOLS

These guides will assist the reader in identifying and using resources found in libraries. In addition, several will help the reader develop appropriate research strategies when looking for information. These tools may be essential when developing research and information seeking skills.

Business Information Sources

Rev ed. Berkeley, CA: University of California Press, 1985.

Public administrators will find this most important annotated bibliography of business reference sources useful for its discussion of methods of finding facts and identification of basic time-saving sources. In addition, public administrators will find citations to important publications in the many fields encountered on a day to day basis, such as statistics, accounting and human resources and personnel management. There is one chapter with citations to sources concerning the "Management of Public and Nonprofit Organizations". The annotations are useful. The work includes a combined author, title and subject index. Lorna M. Daniells is the editor.

How to Find the Law

7th ed. St. Paul, MN: West Publishing Co., 1976.

Although primarily designed as a legal research teaching tool, Morris L. Cohen's *How to Find the Law* may be used as a guide to the major legal service publications and case law tools. It is more than a bibliography; it takes the reader through the use of each of the resources and carefully describes how they can be used cooperatively with one another. The other major legal bibliography teaching tool is J. Myron Jacobstein's *Fundamentals of Legal Research*, 3rd ed. (Mineola, NY: Foundation Press, 1985).

Searching the Law

Dobbs Ferry, NY: Transnational Publishers, 1987.

This valuable book, compiled by Edward J. Bander, is organized by subject and includes under each subject the major professional legal services, the loose-leafs, online services, periodicals and introductory and overview books for that topic.

D. RESEARCH CENTERS

Research Centers Directory

12th ed. Detroit, MI: Gale Research Company, 1988. Annual.

A listing of university-related and independent non-profit organizations conducting research in the United States and Canada. Entries identify the name of the research center and then list address and telephone numbers. Entries provide information on the organization's status within a larger unit such as a department within a university, list research activities and fields and also list publications and services. There are several indexes: master name, keyword and acronym; institutional; special capabilities; and subject. The main volumes are supplemented by *New Research Centers* between editions.

State Government Research Directory

Detroit, MI: Gale Research Company, 1987.

Identifies over 800 research efforts being administered by state government agencies. The directory is arranged by state and then by departments within state government. Each citation includes the department, division, name of the research program, address, staffing information, description of the research activity, the program's access to special facilities and publication and information services. There is an index for name, keyword and agency, and another index for subject access to the research programs.

E. LIBRARIES

Subject Collections

6th ed. New York: R.R. Bowker Company, 1985.

This directory identifies comprehensive collections of informational materials and documents, arranged by subject area, and then alphabetically within the subject area by state. A public administrator may use this tool to identify collections on subjects of interest in their fields.

Directory of Federal Libraries

Phoenix, AZ: Oryx Press, 1987.

This publication identifies more than 2,400 libraries serving the Federal government throughout the United States and overseas. Each citation provides an address and telephone number, lists the library administrator, the type of library, the special subject strengths of the library, the information retrieval services available, its policies for circulating materials outside of the library and the provision of reference services. There is a subject index which identifies those libraries with collection concentrations in specific subject areas.

Directory of Government Document Collections & Librarians

5th ed. Washington, DC: Congressional Information Service, Inc., 1987.

This is a valuable resource which identifies collections of state, local, federal and foreign national government documents. The primary section of this directory provides detailed citations, arranged alphabetically by state and municipality, of libraries collecting government documents. Citations include the library's address and telephone number, type of government documents collected, subject specialties, if the library is designated as an official depository and what is acquired. It also identifies key library staff and provides some basic information such as access and use fees. There is a subject and a source (state, federal, etc.) index.

III. PUBLISHING

A. NON-GOVERNMENTAL PUBLISHING

Following are the major tools covering publishing activity in the United States. Half the battle to maintain currency with the information being published in the field is in knowing how to use those resources which will provide information concerning publishing activity.

Books in Print

New York: R.R. Bowker Company. Annual.

This is the most central source of information on books available in print. Separate sets of volumes are arranged by authors, titles and subjects. A seventh volume is devoted to publishers. This tool, found in every library and bookstore, provides adequate level of bibliographic information for locating materials desired through a publisher, bookstore or library. *Books in Print* also has a mid-year *Supplement* of titles, authors and subjects between editions and other subsidiary products such as *Forthcoming Books. BOOKS IN PRINT* is available online through BRS, Dialog and others, with the online file incorporating all supplements and subsidiary products including out-of-print and out-of-stock titles since 1979.

Literary Market Place

New York: R.R. Bowker Company. Annual.

Known also as *LMP*, this is a directory of the major companies in the media business, including book publishers, radio and television and newspaper publishing. This tool can be useful to the public administrator when trying to identify which companies publish information in a particular subject area. For example, one index is a list of book publishers classified by subject matter. One of the subject areas covered is public administration and urban studies. Another is management.

Irregular Serials & Annuals 1987-88

13th ed. New York: R.R. Bowker Company, 1987.

Lists irregular serials (such as conference proceedings and books published under a series title) and annuals from around the world. This particular resource is arranged alphabetically by subject and then by title of the serial or annual. It is available online with *Ulrich's International Periodicals Directory.*

Standard Periodical Directory

New York: Oxbridge Communications, Inc., 1989. Biennial.

This directory lists periodicals published in the United States and Canada, useful in identifying periodicals by subject area. Arranged by subject headings, each entry lists the title of the periodical and then provides the address of the publisher, lists the editor, gives a short description of the purpose of the periodical, the date it began publication, and then provides the cost. Entries may also include information on frequency and circulation. There is a publication title index.

Ulrich's International Periodicals Directory 1988-89

27th ed. New York: R.R. Bowker Company, 1988.

A listing of 108,950 titles published from all over the world. This three volume resource is arranged alphabetically by subject headings. Within the subject headings, the publications are arranged alphabetically by title. Each entry lists the year publication began, frequency, costs and address and circulation information. Volume 3 provides indexes. It is available online as *ULRICH'S* which incorporates *Irregular Serials and Annuals* and *Ulrich's Update.* All libraries will have this major directory.

B. FEDERAL PUBLISHING

The various levels of government in the United States publish some of the most important and useful information available to public administration practitioners, researchers and students. Governmental bodies, for a variety of reasons, tend to be prolific publishers. In some cases, the only information available on a particular topic will have been published by a local, state or federal government agency. This section describes several of the more important sources which assist in locating and using governmental publications.

CIS/Index

Washington, DC: Congressional Information Service, Inc. Monthly.

This index cumulates quarterly and, along with the abstracts, annually. CIS catalogs, abstracts and indexes all publications issued by the U.S. Congress. Accessing the abstracts is usually accomplished through the index which includes personal name, subject and agency or other organizational name. Each index citation includes a alphanumeric code which corresponds to the abstracts which are in a separate volume by code number. The abstract provides a short description of the congressional committee publication. Additional information identifies the witnesses and includes a short description of the content of their statements and discussion. Abstracts of committee reports include the members' recommendations.

Government Reference Serials

Englewood, CO: Libraries Unlimited, Inc., 1988.

This guide, compiled by LeRoy C. Schwarzkopf, provides bibliographic and descriptive information on the latest edition of each serial title, arranged within subject headings. Annotations are lengthy and usually include a history of the serial. Title and subject indexes are included.

A "serial" is the librarian's name for publications in a series with annual or biannual or triennial, etc., frequency. They use "periodical" if the frequency is greater.

Government Reports Announcement & Index

Washington, DC: U.S. Department of Commerce, National Technical Information Service (NTIS). Biweekly.

NTIS is the central source for the public sale of U.S. government-sponsored research, development and engineering reports and for sales of foreign technical reports and other analyses prepared by national and local government agencies and their contractors or grantees. Most of the citations are to reports which are scientific or technical. There are several categories and subcategories which may be generally useful to public administrators, including Administration and Management, Civil Engineering, Health Care, Problem-Solving Information for State & Local Governments, Transportation and Urban and Regional Technology and Development. Subcategories include: Personnel Management; Public Administration & Government; Education; Building Standards & Codes; Computer Hardware; Metropolitan Rail Transportation; and Housing.

Full bibliographic citations will provide the user with the necessary information to locate a copy of the document. Most importantly, each citation includes an abstract of the report. Indexes, giving the item number of the abstracted bibliographic citation, are: keyword; personal author; corporate author; contract/grant number; and NTIS order/report number. All of the indexes are cumulated annually into a multi-volume publication titled *Government Reports Annual Index*.

See the treatment of *NTIS* in Part 5, ONLINE SERVICES.

Guide to U.S. Government Directories, 1970-1980

Phoenix, AZ: Oryx Press, 1981

Guide to U.S. Government Directories, 1980-1984

Phoenix, AZ: Oryx Press, 1985.

These two publications list directories published by the federal government. The user, once they have the directory cited by this publication in hand, will find the substantive information. Both volumes include a subject index.

Guide to U.S. Government Publications

McLean, VA: Documents Index, 1987.

An annotated listing of important serials and periodicals published by the various departments and agencies of the federal government. Its scope makes this an important work. It lists the important publications of defunct agencies as well as those in existence. There are title and agency indexes. The editor is John L. Andriot; this work is sometimes know to librarians as *Andriot*.

Historic Documents of 19--

Washington, DC: Congressional Quarterly Inc. Annual

A publication beginning in 1972 that includes the text of speeches, court decisions, reports and other original information sources from around the world. The documents are arranged chronologically and each is preceded by a brief introductory paragraph to set it in context. A five year cumulative index is included in each volume with personal name and subject access. This annual cumulation of important documents from each specific year will become more important in time as other sources which contain the same documents become more difficult to locate and use.

Index to U.S. Government Periodicals

New York: Infordata International Inc. Quarterly.

Published quarterly and cumulated annually, this resource indexes articles in over one hundred and eighty federal government periodicals. The index is a combined author, agency and subject listing of bibliographic citations identifying author, title of the article, publication, issue and page numbers, and indicates the inclusion of illustrations, bibliography, etc., in the article. Many of the periodicals have been filmed and are available for sale from microfilm publishers.

Introduction to United States Public Documents

3rd ed. Littleton, CO: Libraries Unlimited, Inc., 1983.

An account of the basic sources of information of the structure of federal government publications. After an overview of public documents, the author explores the Government Printing Office, Superintendent of Documents, the depository library system, technical report literature, selected information sources for federal government publications, legislative branch materials, publications of the presidency, selected categories of executive branch and independent agency publications and sources of legal information. Most sources are briefly annotated with their legal authority often cited. There is a selected title and series index and a subject and name index.

Locating United States Government Information

Buffalo, NY: William S. Hein & Company, 1983.

This is a useful introductory guidebook explaining how to locate information within the federal government. It treats the Superintendent of Documents classification system, government comprehensive indexes and the commercial Congressional Information Service indexes and indexes and guides to legislation and regulations. There are chapters on locating statistics, census information, technical reports and maps and audiovisual materials. The author, Edward Herman, also shows readers how to trace a bill through Congress and how to use the Freedom of Information and Privacy Acts to obtain information.

There is an annotated bibliography near the end of this work which discusses the major information sources concerning publication of information. A supplemental chart-like presentation is useful. A combined title and subject index is included in this important guide.

The Investigative Reporters and Editors, Inc. has a more specialized and more thorough tool on the Freedom of Information Act and document acquisition titled *The Reporter's Handbook; an Investigator's Guide to Documents and Techniques* (N.Y.: St. Martin's Press, 1983).

Monthly Catalog of United States Government Publications

Washington, DC: U.S. Government Printing Office. Monthly.

Cumulated annually, this publication is designed to be the definitive source of information on the numerous publications by the federal government. The main part of the Catalog is arranged alphabetically by executive department and then further subdivided by departments and agencies. Congressional committees and independent agency publications are also listed. The citations resemble the information a user would see on a library card catalog. Although the citations are not annotated, extensive notes and subject headings for the publication may provide some hints to the reader as to the documents contents. Information is also provided so that the reader may order the item or ascertain its availability from a federal depository library. The *Monthly Catalog* utilizes several indexes: author; title; subject; series and report; and title and keyword. Inexpensive machine-readable access to the Catalog is also available in many libraries.

A fifteen volume set has been published titled *Cumulative Subject Index to the Monthly Catalog of United States*

Government Publications 1900-1971. The more recent Monthly Catalog is usually searched as an online file: *GPO MONTHLY CATALOG* from BRS and Dialog. *GPO PUBLICATIONS REFERENCE FILE* is the online catalog of documents currently on sale from the Government Printing Office. It is available only online or on microfiche.

Microfilmed or paper copies of the documents are available at selected federal government depository libraries.

Popular Names of U.S. Government Reports

4th ed. Washington, DC: Library of Congress, 1984.

A catalog of federal reports arranged by their popular name. Many Congressional Committee reports are known by their primary author although the Committee is listed as the main author. Information in each citation is that of a library catalog card prepared by the Library of Congress. There is a subject and corporate entry index.

Subject Guide to Major United States Government Publications

2nd ed. Chicago, IL: American Library Association, 1987.

This presents briefly annotated lists of major federal publications arranged by subject. It also includes an annotated bibliography of guides, catalogs, indexes and directories on federal publications.

Subject Guide to U.S. Government Reference Sources

Littleton, CO: Libraries Unlimited, Inc., 1985.

This annotated bibliography of federal government reference publications can be a useful tool for the public administrator beginning a search for information which may have been published by the federal government. Citations are organized under type of material, such as General Works, Handbooks, etc.

Tapping the Government Grapevine: The User-Friendly Guide to U.S. Government Information Sources

Phoenix, AZ: Oryx Press, 1988.

This provides narrative explanations of sources and includes bibliographic citations to important reference tools such as directories, indexes and bibliographies. There is discussion of: depository libraries; scientific information; patents, trademarks and copyrights; legislative information; regulations; executive branch information; judicial information; statistics; and foreign and international documents, among other informational sources. The compiler is Judith Schiek Robinson.

Using Government Publications

Phoenix, AZ: Oryx Press, 1985.

This two volume work may be very important to public administrators in identifying and illustrating various searching strategies useful in locating information contained in government publications. The work is divided into subject areas such as Business Aids and Agriculture. The authors illustrate four search strategies and discuss their implementation: subject; agency; statistical; and special techniques.

C. STATE PUBLISHING

A Bibliography of State Bibliographies, 1970-1982

Littleton, CO: Libraries Unlimited, Inc., 1985.

An annotated bibliography of over 1,000 bibliographies published by state governments on selected subject areas. This resource is arranged alphabetically by state and then alphabetically by subject area. Thirty-nine broad subject areas are covered, such as agriculture, disabled, employment, health, libraries, planning, safety and wetlands. The citations identify the state publisher of the bibliography. Addresses of the publishers are included in an easy to use appendix. Separate indexes are included for titles of publications and subjects.

Guide to State Legislative Materials

3rd ed. Littleton, CO: Fred B. Rothman & Co., 1985.

A looseleaf resource of the American Association of Law Libraries, this guide provides, by state, information on sources of state legislative and administrative documents. Each state section includes information on bills, hearings, legislative digest, committee reports, debates, journals and proceedings, legislative manual or directory, slip laws, session laws, codes, legislative pamphlet service, advance annotation service to codes, bar association legislative recommendations, Attorney General opinions, Executive Orders, administrative regulations and state law guides. A narrative is also included which clarifies and expands upon the information included in the state entry. Addresses and telephone numbers for key providers of state legislative and administrative information completes each entry.

Two appendixes are helpful. One is a list, with addresses, of publishers of state legislative information. Another identifies commercial companies providing services which monitor state legislation and regulations.

Monthly Checklist of State Publications

Washington, DC: Exchange and Gift Division Processing Services, Library of Congress. Monthly.

This is a resource for identifying state publications received by the Library of Congress from state agencies. Although it is not exhaustive because of requirements imposed by the Library of Congress, and because many state agencies do not forward their publications to the Library of Congress, it is still one of the few reference tools that provide this informational access. The Checklist is arranged alphabetically by state and then by issuing agency. Separate sections are included after the states for publications of associations of state officials and regional organizations; and another is provided for surveys, studies, manuals and reports issued by state libraries. Entries contain complete bibliographic citations; they are assigned subject headings as appropriate and are sometimes assigned a Library of Congress accession number. Periodicals are listed semiannually with a cumulation in the December issue. There is a subject index at the end of each monthly publication. A cumulative annual subject and issuing agency index is published.

State Government Reference Publications: An Annotated Bibliography

2nd ed. Littleton, CO: Libraries Unlimited, Inc., 1981.

David W. Parish's work is useful as a tool to locate state publishers of information. Each citation is briefly but adequately annotated. Chapters include: Official State Bibliography; Blue Books, which are general information sources from state governments; Legislative Manuals; State Government Finances; Statistical Abstracts and Other Data Sources; Directories; Tourist Guides; Audiovisual Guides, Atlases and Maps; Bibliographies and General References. The appendix, "A Subject Core of State Publications," can be useful to familiarize users with the possibilities of state documents. Other appendixes include suggested readings, reference tools, a subject guide to state publications and agency addresses.

State Legislative Sourcebook

Topeka, KS: Government Research Service, 1988. Loose-leaf.

An important and well organized source of information on each of the state legislatures. The intent of the publication is to explain what information is available in that state and how to get it. Each state chapter begins with a section on "Legislative Organization and Process" which includes general information and then provides critical annotated citations to sources on: how a bill becomes law; books on legislative organization and politics; leadership and committee rosters; House and Senate rules; legislator information including directories, biographical profiles and financial information; session information including official legislative documents, bill status and reporting services and session summary information; interim study period information; lobbying information; and general state government information including "Blue" books and reference publications, books on state government and politics, newspapers, journals, newsletters registers, etc., and state government telephone directories.

The appendices also contain much useful information. Appendix A identifies addresses and telephone numbers of sources for information on bill status. Appendix B has the same information on bill rooms or document rooms for each state legislature. The next appendix is a bibliography of books and articles on the state legislatures and the art of influencing them. Sources identified discuss such topics as: the legislative organization, procedures and process and life in the legislature; interest groups; election campaign techniques and financing; lobbying; public affairs and governmental relation functions; bill introduction and tracking services; and general state government and politics. The last section of this appendix describes ten national political organizations of various political and philosophical leanings.

Subject Compilations of State Laws

Westport, CT: Greenwood Press, 1981.

Subject Compilations of State Laws, 1979-1983

Westport, CT: Greenwood Press, 1984.

Subject Compilations of State Laws, 1983-1985

Urbana, IL: Carol Boast and Cheryl Nyberg, 1985.

These volumes are essentially annotated bibliographies of sources which include, or are themselves, compilations of citations to state laws. The main body of each volume is the annotated bibliography which is arranged by subject. Bibliographic citations are complete. Library of Congress classification numbers are included to facilitate library access. Resources covered by this invaluable source book includes monographs, court decisions, law review articles, journals and other serials. The annotation refers the reader to the exact page, footnote, table, or part of the publication which contains the citation. Each volume includes an author index and a publisher index.

Although the volumes were completed by different authors and different publishers, the annotated bibliographies and citations do not duplicate the preceding volumes. In fact, each successive volume builds upon its predecessor, with the citation numbering and subject headings systems developed for the first work utilized by the subsequent volumes. Some 4,200 individual subject compilations of state laws have been located among the three publications.

D. MUNICIPAL PUBLISHING

Index to Current Urban Documents

Westport, CT: Greenwood Press. Quarterly. Annual.

This is a useful resource for public administrators wanting to locate local government documents. It has been published since 1973. Local libraries, government units and civic and research organizations of nearly 300 of the largest cities and counties forward copies of local government publications to the publisher who prepares the Index and microfilms a majority of the documents received. Subscribers may use several option plans provided by the publisher to order microfiche copies of documents.

Simple to use, the Index is composed of bibliographic citations in two indexes: geographic and subject. The geographic index is arranged alphabetically by the municipality or county (not by state) and then by the departmental name. The subject index includes cross-references. One document may appear under as many as twelve subject headings. The bibliographic citations are more complete in the geographic index.

Municipal Government Reference Sources

New York: R.R. Bowker Company, 1978.

Arranged by state and then by community, this source lists and annotates municipal documents. Most of the municipalities covered exceed 100,000 in population, or the two largest cities in the state if none exceeded the 100,000 level. Several cities which met this criteria did not report. There is a county-city cross reference appendix and a subject index.

Part 4
PUBLIC ADMINISTRATION PERIODICALS

Articles on subjects relevant to public administration appear in a very large number of newsletters, magazines, academic journals and law reviews. In order to make access to this information easier, we have done the following:

1. Described those abstracting services we have used and identified which services cover each periodical;

2. Listed the major services which do only subject indexing of periodicals;

3. Identified a group of periodicals which are accessible and have some impact on the public administration audience in the United States;

4. Identified the tools which comprehensively list periodicals in print and give publishing information, contact and price;

5. Identified periodicals by subject in the SUBJECT INDEX at the back of this *Desk Book.*

I. ABSTRACTING SERVICES

Acquiring copies of articles often involves trips to various libraries, extensive photocopying, the use of your library's InterLibrary Loan. Or it may involve the expense of an article delivery service such as University Microfilms International's (UMI's) Article Clearinghouse. Reading an abstract or summary of the article can often tell you, beforehand, whether it is worth acquiring a copy of the article. Often you will need no more information then that contained in a good, substantive abstract. The *UMI Article Clearinghouse Catalog*, which includes all but a very few specialized practitioner journals listed here, is available by phone at (800) 732-0616. This is a source of photocopies of articles within 48 hours. Articles may be ordered by phone or online by computer.

See Part 5, ONLINE SERVICES, for description of the online database producers and the retailers of online databases. Their products include all the major abstracting services described below and they also provide full-text service for many periodicals.

ABI/INFORM

Online from Data Courier; available through BRS, Dialog, NEXIS, and others.

This covers 800 business and related publications. The abstracts attempt to get across the major substantive content of the article, not simply indicate what it is about. Their coverage includes the major national and international public administration periodicals. *ABI/INFORM*, including the article summaries, is also available on CD-ROM where the last 5 years can be searched without online costs.

Abstract Newsletter: Administration and Management

A weekly from the U.S. National Technical Information Service (NTIS).

This and the following two newsletters are generated out of the NTIS database which covers government-sponsored research and analyses prepared by or for federal agencies. The database supports the public distribution of reports available from federal government departments. You may find this weekly newsletter of considerable value; however, an occasional online use of the NTIS database may be more cost effective.

Abstract Newsletter: Problem-Solving Information for State and Local Governments

A weekly published by the U.S. National Technical Information Service.

Abstract Newsletter: Health Care

A weekly from the U.S. National Technical Information Service.

Educational Administration Abstracts

A quarterly from the University Council for Educational Administration and Washington University.

This covers about 150 journals of interest to practicing administrators.

HEALTH PLANNING & ADMINISTRATION

Online from the U.S. National Library of Medicine; available through BRS, Dialog, and others.

This database covers the nonclinical literature on health service planning, financial management, personnel, etc. contained in the NLM's database *MEDLINE* and the American Hospital Association's *Hospital Literature Index* and some additional journals. Not every item will have an abstract available. It is an inexpensive and very useful online service for this area.

Human Resources Abstracts

A quarterly from Sage Publications, Inc.

This abstracts journals dealing with manpower, human resources, and related policy questions. This is perhaps the single best inexpensive publication for its coverage of a broad range of public administration topics.

Journal of Economic Literature

A quarterly from the American Economic Association. Online as ECONOMIC LITERATURE INDEX from Dialog and others.

This is a journal (and in an expanded form, an online service) which publishes ten or so scholarly articles each year; however, the journal is devoted primarily to book reviews, annotations on new books, printing the table of contents of major scholarly journals in economics, and to selected 100 word abstracts of articles in economic journals. The online file also includes indexing in *Index of Economic Articles*, another publication of the Association. It is useful for the scholarly literature of the economics profession and covers only those public administration topics studied by economists such as fiscal theory and policy, the economic effects of regulation, privatization, manpower training and social service program economics, etc.

NTIS

An online database from the National Technical Information Services.

The citations are to research and development report literature sponsored in whole or part by federal government agencies. The accompaning abstracts only indicate the scope of the work cited. *NTIS* covers material from 1964 (Dialog) or 1970 (BRS), some two million records. Therefore, it is useful to do a brief, preliminary search. The end user should study the results of this first search and then search again. In a study of searches in 55 databases (*Online Review*, April, 1988) for topics in urban and regional planning, NTIS usually had the most online "hits." It does not usually provide the largest number of useful citations.

The full documents are available from NTIS and may be ordered online.

Personnel Management Abstracts

A quarterly from Personnel Management Abstracts.

This identifies by subject category the contents of ninety-two journals, both academic and practitioner, and provides abstracts. Ten or more books are also abstracted in each issue.

PROMT

An online service from Predicast, Inc.; available through BRS and Dialog.

Business and management publications, including major public administration titles, are covered with substantive abstracts. Predicast, Inc. is a major provider of business information, including trade, industry and social statistics. Like *ABI/INFORM*, it provides well written, substantive abstracts; many include tables of data.

Psychological Abstracts

A monthly from the American Psychological Association. Available online as PsycINFO through BRS, Dialog, and others.

Among the more than 1,300 journals, dissertations and reports covered are most of the public administration scholarly journals. Because of the very large number of journals this service covers, and because of the thousands of dissertations (for which abstracts are not provided), it is best to use the print service first to learn the appropriate index terms or key words used by *PsycINFO* for your topic. Then search online.

Sage Public Administration Abstracts

A quarterly from Sage Publications, Inc.

This covers articles in 120 periodicals. The list is heavily scholarly and international but also includes some of the best regional and practitioner titles. The service also covers some books and other public administration material.

Sage Urban Studies Abstracts

A quarterly from Sage Publication, Inc.

The source list of this Sage publication is primarily U.S. periodicals. The major planning journals are included, as is *Baseline Data Reports*. This would be the second choice, after *Human Resources Abstracts*, for the small public administration library.

Social Planning, Policy and Development Abstracts

An online subfile from Sociological Abstracts available separately from BRS.

This subfile provides indexing and abstracts of the more practical, problem-solving literature of Sociology while *Sociological Abstracts* itself presents the more theoretical or methodological professional literature.

Sociological Abstracts (SA)

Published five time a year by Sociological Abstracts, Inc. and co-sponsored by the International Sociological Association. Available online from Dialog.

This is the major abstracting tool in Sociology; it is international and is not limited to English for the more than 1,600 journals it screens for material which will be indexed and abstracted. The service also covers association and conference papers, books and book reviews. Since the printed alphabetic subject index is extensive, the user might find the subject categories in each issue a useful approach. The sister publication *Social Planning, Policy and Development Abstracts* also may be useful. *SA* may also be searched online and this is the most efficient method for a precise search, one not requiring browsing.

Social Work Research & Abstracts

A quarterly from the National Association of Social Workers.

This is the major abstracting service for this field covering all of the social work journals and related publications including dissertations. The periodical also publishes original research. It is available online from BRS.

Urban Affairs Abstracts

A weekly from the National League of Cities.

The most timely and comprehensive of the abstracting services covering urban affairs. The National League of Cities operates an online database service directly, rather than through a database retailer such as Dialog, which provides full-text search access to *Urban Affairs Abstracts* as well as to their other information services.

United States Political Science Documents

An annual from the NASA Industrial Applications Center, University of Pittsburgh. Also available online through BRS, Dialog and others.

Emphasis is on scholarly articles on foreign policy, international relations and behavioral sciences, but among the 150 periodicals covered are a number devoted to public administration.

Work Related Abstracts

A monthly looseleaf publication from Harmonie Park Press.

This service is not well indexed for public adminis- tration topics; however, it covers labor relations articles well and provides brief one sentence abstracts. It alone covers union publications.

II. INDEXING SERVICES

The following are indexing services. They do not provide abstracts of books or articles but only subject indexing and citations. Always prefer an abstracting service, if there is one which fits your information needs, and take advantage of the summaries of articles and content notes on books. However, the subject indexes are useful if what you need is precisely the quick assistance in article chasing they provide. Searches using the online indexing services will be more comprehensive and will be more cost effective, if your time is a cost factor.

Accountant's Index

A quarterly from the American Institute of Certified Public Accountants (AICPA).

Indexing to 290 English language accounting periodicals in quarterly and annual print volumes. Mead Data's LEXIS/NEXIS provides an online access to this index and to all the major accounting literature.

Alternative Press Index

A quarterly from Alternative Center Press.

Indexing to 150 journals which have significant circulation but are mostly not indexed elsewhere. Mostly they are left, liberal, libertarian, or muck-raking magazines.

CSI/Federal Index

A monthly from National Standards Association.

Indexing to U.S. legal, regulatory and judicial information in the *Federal Register*, *Congressional Record*, *Compilation of Presidential Documents* and *U.S. Law Week*. Also available online.

Current Law Index

A monthly, with annual cumulation, from Information Access Company; Co-sponsor: American Association of Law Libraries.

Subject and case indexes to the principle legal periodicals. See *Legal Resource Index.*

General Periodical Index; Academic Library Edition

Machine-based indexing from Information Access Company.

Also known by its former name, *InfoTrac*, this provides subject indexing to over 900 business press titles and over 300 selected academic and general interest periodicals. It is widely available in public and academic libraries and is very useful for finding citations to public administration topics. Information Access Company also produces indexing and some full-text services which are available online through Dialog including *NEWSEARCH* and *TRADE AND INDUSTRY INDEX*. This product is now providing an increasing number of article abstracts; but it is not yet an abstracting service.

Index to Current Urban Documents

A quarterly from Greenwood Press.

This functions as an index to a collection of municipal documents maintained by Greenwood's Urban Documents Center, (203) 226-3571, at Westport, CT and marketed to libraries as a microfiche collection. There is broad subject indexing of this material, but most will use the city by city arrangement listing the publications received and reproduced in the film collection.

Index to U.S. Government Periodicals

A quarterly from Infordata.

Subject indexing to over 100 periodicals published by federal government agencies. While covering only a small portion of government agency magazines, this is a very useful index. It does not include Federal Reserve bank periodicals.

Index to Legal Periodicals

Monthly from H.W. Wilson Co.

This provides subject indexing and is published in paper with an annual cumulation. It is also available online and in CD-ROM form. The online product, available from H.W. Wilson only and the CD-ROM product may be searched by author, journal and title words. The product covers about 500 legal periodicals.

Index to Periodical Articles Related to Law

Granville Publishers, Inc.

This provides indexing of journals not included in the *Index to Legal Periodicals*.

Legal Resource Index

Information Access Company; Co-sponsor: American Association of Law Libraries.

Indexing coverage of *Current Law Index* plus about 150 additional legal journals and newspapers and some legal newsletters and association publications. The product is available on microfilm and on CD-ROM as *LegalTrac*. Online it is available from Dialog and NEXIS/LEXIS. Online it is searchable by any item in the citation: title words, author, case and indexing terms, etc., and with complex searches employing "and," "or," and "not." This index also covers the major public administration periodicals where, as with many of the abstracting and indexing services mentioned here, nearly half the citations are to international public administration topics.

PAIS Bulletin

A monthly updated annual cumulation from Public Affairs Information Service, Inc.

This can be found in many libraries. It is a subject index to selected articles in selected periodicals, to selected governmental publications and to some miscellaneous pamphlets. It can be useful as a supplement to other indexes but use other indexes or abstracting services first if they are available.

Shepard's Law Review Citations

A bimonthly from Shepard's / McGraw Hill

Indexing to about 180 law reviews and legal periodicals. In addition to finding articles by subject, you may "Shepardize" them, that is, find every time a law review article has been cited by the courts or in other articles.

Social Science Index

Quarterly from H.W. Wilson, Inc.

Indexing of a selection of the major social science journals including several on public administration. H.W. Wilson also publishes a *General Science Index* which can be useful for its coverage of medical, environmental and other science-related topics. Most public and university libraries will have the Wilson indexes and many subscribe to all the periodicals so indexed.

Social Science Citation Index

Published three times a year from Institute for Scientific Information.

The special indexing coverage of over 4,000 science and social science journals make this product and its companion, *Science Citation Index*, unique. There is an author index, a corporate index by author's affiliation, an index by key terms in the author's title, and a citation index by authors of articles cited by others. This last index allows you to "Shepardize" science and social science articles. Both *SSCI* and *SCI* are available online. These products are primarily citators, such as Shepard's, and are not comparable to the easy-to-use indexes.

III. SELECTED PUBLIC ADMINISTRATION PERIODICALS

You can expect major libraries to have all but a few of these periodicals; any library which uses a national computerized cataloging system (and most do) will to be able to easily acquire copies of articles through the American Library Association's InterLibrary Loan (ILL) procedures. The library's ILL services are not generally available to undergraduate students for course-assigned research.

Administration and Society

A quarterly from Sage Publications, Inc.

Articles on public and human service organizations and their administrative processes. Abstracted in International Political Science Abstracts, Personnel Literature, Sage Public Administration Abstracts, Sage Urban Studies Abstracts.

Administration in Social Work

A quarterly from Haworth Press, Inc.

Abstracted in Human Resources Abstracts, Psychological Abstracts, Sociological Abstracts.

Administrative Law Review

A quarterly from the American Bar Association, Section of Administrative Law.

Scholarly articles, seminar reports and speeches dealing with the administration of federal agencies and departments. Indexed in the legal periodical indexes.

Administrative Science Quarterly

A quarterly from Cornell University, Johnson Graduate School of Management.

A major journal for the academic discipline of public administration; empirical studies, theoretical articles, review articles. Abstracted in ABI/INFORM, Economic Abstracts, Educational Administration Abstracts, International Political Science Abstracts, MANAGEMENT CONTENTS, Personnel Management Abstracts, Personnel Literature, PROMT, Psychological Abstracts, Sage Public Administration Abstracts, Social Work Research & Abstracts, Sociological Abstracts.

American Academy of Political and Social Science. Annals

A bimonthly from the American Academy of Political and Social Science. Publisher: Sage Publications, Inc.

Each single-topic issue is focused on an issue in American politics. Articles are written at the invitation of the editor. Abstracted in Human Resources Abstracts, Personnel Literature, Sage Urban Studies Abstracts, Social Work Research & Abstracts.

American Business Law Journal

A quarterly from American Business Law Association.

Articles on business law and public responsibility. Abstracted in MANAGEMENT CONTENTS and TRADE AND INDUSTRY INDEX. Indexed in the law and the business periodical indexes.

American City & County; Administration, Engineering, and Operations in Relation to Local Government

A monthly from Communication Channels, Inc.

A practitioner journal. It includes several public works special features (buying guides, salary surveys, conventions, surveys of city and county administrators). Abstracted in Chemical Abstracts, INSPEC, Oceanic Abstracts, Pollution Abstracts, Select Water Research Abstracts, TRADE & INDUSTRY INDEX, and others.

American Demographics

A monthly from American Demographics, Inc.

Articles on consumer demographics by professionals in the field of demographics. The publisher also produces a *Guide to Demographic Data Sources* (only a current edition will be useful) and a *Directory of Microcomputer Data and Software for Demographic Analysis*. Available full-text online from Dow Jones News Retrieval. Abstracted in PROMT and indexed in the business press indexes.

American Journal of Political Science

A quarterly from the Midwest Political Science Association.

Abstracted in International Political Science Abstracts, Sage Public Administration Abstracts, Sage Urban Studies Abstracts.

American Political Science Review

A quarterly from the American Political Science Association.

As the official journal of the Association, this scholarly journal's articles represent the current concerns and methods dominant in the Association. Abstracted in International Political Science Abstracts, Personnel Literature, Sage Public Administration Abstracts and most online services.

American Politics Quarterly

A quarterly published by Sage Publications, Inc.

Abstracted in America History & Life, International Political Science Abstracts and the Sage abstracting publications.

American Review of Public Administration

A quarterly from the University of Missouri, Kansas City.

For scholars and practitioners, articles view public administration topics from the field. Abstracted in ABI/INFORM, Personnel Literature, Sage Public Administration Abstracts, and others.

Baseline Data Report

A bimonthly from International City Management Association.

Reports, usually including survey data, for the manager. Abstracted in Sage Public Administration Abstracts.

Bureaucrat

A quarterly from Bureaucrat, Inc.

Practitioner-oriented articles on a wide range of subjects: business law and public responsibility, office administration. Emphasis on alternative solutions. Abstracted in ABI/INFORM, Human Resources Abstracts, MANAGEMENT CONTENTS, Sage Public Administration Abstracts, U.S. Political Science Documents, Urban Affairs Abstracts.

California Journal

A monthly from California Journal, Inc.

Abstracted in Sage Public Administration Abstracts, Sage Urban Studies Abstracts.

City and State

A tabloid monthly from Crain Communications.

The subject here is public administration finance news. The major advertisers are investment firms handling public bonds, bond insurers, trust banks, etc. A regular feature is a ranking of municipal bond underwriters by dollar share of the municipal bond market.

City Almanac

A quarterly from New School for Social Research, Center for New York City Affairs.

Each issue presents a thorough background article on an issue effecting New York City then brief items present points of view, proposed solutions, etc. Special features cover services and the city economy. Abstracted in Sage Public Administration Abstracts.

City Hall Digest

A monthly from City Hall Communications.

Serves as an information exchange for municipal officials describing special programs. Abstracted in Urban Affairs Abstracts.

Columbia Journal of Law and Social Problems

A quarterly from Columbia University, School of Law.

An academic journal addressing issues of new and changing legislation and the social impact of law. Abstracted in Human Resources Abstracts and covered by the legal periodical indexes.

Community Development Journal

A quarterly from Oxford University Press.

Abstracted in Human Resources Abstracts, Sage Public Administration Abstracts, Social Work Research & Abstracts, Sociological Abstracts.

Computers, Environment and Urban Systems

A quarterly from Pergamon Press, Inc., Journals Division.

Abstracted in Psychological Abstracts (PsycINFO), Sage Public Administration Abstracts, Sage Urban Studies Abstracts.

Congress and the Presidency

A semiannual from American University, Center for Congressional and Presidential Studies.

Abstracted in International Political Science Abstracts.

Congressional Quarterly Service. Weekly Report

A weekly from Congressional Quarterly, Inc.

A weekly summary of congressional activities with reports and special sections on major legislative areas, voting records and other special features and indexes. This weekly, and many other publications from Congressional Quarterly, Inc., should be considered for a public administration library. It is self-indexed and cumulated.

Contemporary Policy Issues

A quarterly from Western Economic Association International.

Abstracted in Human Resources Abstracts, Journal of Economic Literature, Sage Public Administration Abstracts.

CSG Backgrounder

A monthly from the States Information Center of the Council of State Governments.

This publication identifies and briefly discusses the pros and cons of issues of concern to state government. Each monthly report is on a specific topic. This is not indexed in the national indexes but a cumulative index, back to 1981, is included in each issue.

Current Municipal Problems

A quarterly, with annual cumulation, from Callaghan & Co.

In any context where any one of the practitioner-oriented municipal magazines is read, this publication will be a valuable addition. It reprints articles selected from these magazines nationwide, about 100 per year. Many of the articles would, otherwise, remain inaccessible. Indexed in NEWSEARCH and the legal periodical indexes and held in most law libraries.

Editorial Research Reports

A weekly from Congressional Quarterly, Inc.

Each 10 or 12 page report is on a specific topic providing a status report, data, and a pro and con analysis by commentators in the field. It is cumulated annually in a bound volume which includes an index of 10 years of reports.

Employee Benefit Plan Review

A monthly from Charles D. Spencer & Associates.

A major journal on this subject and especially valuable for any library which regularly uses a major labor and employment benefit loose-leaf services.

Abstracted in MANAGEMENT CONTENTS, Personnel Literature and covered in the business indexes.

Employee Relations Law Journal

A quarterly from Executive Enterprises, Inc.

Articles on business law, personnel and labor relations. Abstracted in ABI\INFORM, Human Relations Abstracts, MANAGEMENT CONTENTS, TRADE AND INDUSTRY INDEX, and the legal indexing services.

Environment and Behavior

A bimonthly from the Environmental Design Research Association; published by Sage Publications, Inc.

Scholarly articles on the human impact of environmental developments and decisions. Abstracted in Psychological Abstracts, Sage Urban Studies Abstracts, Sociological Abstracts and covered by the medical and other indexing services.

Environment and Planning C: Government & Policy

A quarterly from Pion Ltd., London.

A scholarly international journal in which articles feature statistical analysis. Abstracted in Human Relations Abstracts, Sage Public Administration Abstracts, Sage Urban Studies Abstracts.

Evaluation and Program Planning

A quarterly from Pergamon Press, Inc.

Abstracted in Human Relations Abstracts, Psyc-INFO, Sociological Abstracts, and a number of health literature indexing and abstracting services.

Evaluation Practice

A quarterly from the American Evaluation Association; published by Sage Publications, Inc.

This was a news publication of the association until

recently. As generally, "evaluation" in the title refers to systematic and quantitative appraisals of social programs. The federal government funds a good deal of research into the impact of its programs and this and other "evaluation" journals report on that activity.

Evaluation Review

Published six time a year by Sage Publications, Inc.

Published scholarly appraisals of social programs. Abstracted in Human Relations Abstracts, PsycINFO, Sage Public Administration Abstracts, Sociological Abstracts and the health and criminal justice literature indexing and abstracting services.

Facts on File

A weekly from Facts on File, Inc.

This is a news digest compiled from newspapers and government documents. It is international and a good source for recently published statistical and financial information not included or covered by the other weekly news publications. Sources are not usually cited. It is not indexed separately but includes its own indexing.

Federal Reserve Bulletin

A monthly from the Board of Governors of the Federal Reserve System.

While *Survey of Current Business* is the most important single source of business statistics, this journal has that position for banking and monetary statistics. The articles in each issue are also of considerable value, as are articles appearing in the numerous reviews and other periodicals from the 12 regional Federal Reserve System banks. This journal is indexed widely, but for access to appropriate articles in the regional bank periodicals you must see *Fed in Print*, published twice a year and distributed free by Information Services and Research Library, Federal Reserve Bank of Philadelphia, (215) 574-6428.

From the State Capitals. Public Employee Policy

A monthly from Wakeman-Walworth, Inc.

This is one of a variety of newsletter publications from this firm reporting news and developments in state programs and legislation. See the list of their newsletters in *National Directory of Newsletters and Reporting Services.*

GAO Journal

A quarterly from the U.S. Government Accounting Office.

Practitioner articles, interviews, reviews and issue survey articles. Abstracted in MANAGEMENT CONTENT, Sage Public Administration Abstracts.

Government Accountants Journal

A quarterly from the Association of Government Accountants.

A practitioner journal of financial management in the public sector. Abstracted in ABI/INFORM, MANAGEMENT CONTENTS.

Government Executive

Published ten times a year by National Journals, Inc.

Abstracted in MANAGEMENT CONTENTS, Personnel Literature, Sage Public Administration Abstracts.

Government Finance Review

A bimonthly from Government Finance Officers Association (GFOA) formerly Municipal Finance Officers Association.

A practitioner journal focused on state, county and local government finance issues and including reports from the association. A valuable feature is the abstracts of new publications added to the GFOA library. Abstracted in MANAGEMENT CONTENTS, PROMT, Sage Public Administration Abstracts, and covered by the business periodical indexes.

Government Product News

A monthly from Penton/IPC Publications.

Includes buyers guides for parks and recreation equipment, grounds and public works equipment, etc. and special features on plant maintenance, budget aids, etc. Abstracted in NEWSEARCH, TRADE & INDUSTRY INDEX.

Government Publications Review

A bimonthly from Pergamon Press, Inc.

Valuable primarily for librarians.

Government Union Review

A quarterly from Public Service Research Foundation.

Articles focus on unionism as a feature of public sector employee relations and cover many issues of labor negotiation. Abstracted in LEGAL RESOURCES INDEX, MANAGEMENT CONTENTS, NEWSEARCH.

Guide to Management Improvement Projects in Local Government

A quarterly from the International City Management Association.

This presents brief abstracts of reports on local projects. Each report usually identifies a local contact person for further information. It is very useful for investigating and importing ideas from other communities. It is not covered by any indexing service.

Group and Organization Studies

A quarterly from the School of Business, State University of New York, Albany.

Articles on organizational behavior and organizational development, personnel and labor relations. Abstracted in ABI/INFORM, MANAGEMENT CONTENTS, PROMPT.

Harvard Business Review

A bimonthly from Harvard University, Graduate School of Business Administration.

A major professional management journal covering all aspects of general management and policy. Abstracted in ABI/INFORM, Human Resources Abstracts, MANAGEMENT CONTENTS, NEWSEARCH, NEXIS, PROMT, and other indexing and abstracting services.

Harvard Civil Rights-Civil Liberties Law Review

Twice a year from Harvard Civil Rights-Civil Liberties Law Review.

Articles dealing with public interest law. Abstracted in Human Resources Abstracts, NEWSEARCH, Sage Urban Studies Abstracts, and covered by the legal periodical indexes.

Human Communication Research

A quarterly from International Communication Association. Publisher: Sage Publications, Inc.

Articles focus on organizational behavior, organizational communication, and personnel. Abstracted in Current Index to Journals in Education (CIJE), Psychological Abstracts, Sage Public Administration Abstracts.

Human Rights Quarterly

From Johns Hopkins University Press.

Perhaps the most scholarly of many journals covering civil liberties and human rights policy; articles here are theoretical and international. Examination of the whole range of periodicals in this area in a university or law library is recommended before selecting those of value in your context. Abstracted in MANAGEMENT CONTENTS.

Industrial Relations Law Journal

A quarterly from the School of Law, University of California, Berkeley, CA.

Publishes scholarly analysis and comment on industrial relations issues; a valuable special feature is abstracts of selected labor relations articles from other journals. Abstracted in ABI/INFORM, MANAGEMENT CONTENTS, NEWSEARCH; indexed in the legal periodical indexes.

International Journal of Government Auditing

A quarterly from International Organization of Supreme Audit Institutions.

Abstracted in ABI/INFORM, MANAGEMENT CONTENTS

International Journal of Public Administration

A quarterly from Marcel Dekker Journals.

American public administration topics primarily. Abstracted in ABI/INFORM, Human Resources Abstracts, MANAGEMENT CONTENTS, Personnel Literature, Sage Public Administration Abstracts, Sage Urban Studies Abstracts.

Journal of Accounting and Public Policy

A quarterly from the College of Business and Management, University of Maryland.

Articles on accounting and public administration. Abstracted in ABI/INFORM, Sage Public Administration Abstracts.

Journal of Collective Negotiations in the Public Sector

A quarterly from Baywood Publishing Co. Inc.

Abstracted in ABI/INFORM, Educational Administration Abstracts., Human Relations Abstracts, MANAGEMENT CONTENTS, Personnel Literature, Work Related Abstracts, and covered by the legal indexing services.

Journal of Community Health

A quarterly from Human Sciences Press, Inc.

Abstracted in HEALTH PLANNING AND ADMINISTRATION and other health literature services, Human Resources Abstracts, Sociological Abstracts.

Journal of Health and Human Resources Administration

A quarterly from Southern Public Administration Foundation, Inc., Publisher: Auburn University at Montgomery.

Abstracted in HEALTH PLANNING AND ADMINISTRATION, MANAGEMENT CONTENTS, Sage Public Administration Abstracts, and other health care indexing services.

Journal of Health Politics, Policy and Law

A quarterly from Duke University, Department of Health Administration.

Abstracted in Biological Abstracts (BIOSIS), Health Planning and Administration, Human Resources Abstracts, International Political Science Abstracts, NEWSEARCH, Sage Public Administration Abstracts, and other health and legal indexing services.

Journal of Human Resources, Education, Manpower and Welfare Economics

A quarterly from the Industrial Relations Research Institute of the University of Wisconsin.

Econometrics articles. Abstracted in ABI/INFORM, Economics Literature Index, Educational Administration Abstracts, Human Resources Abstracts, MANAGEMENT ABSTRACTS, Personnel Literature, Personnel Management Abstracts, Sociological Abstracts, Work Related Abstracts, and others.

Journal of Management

A quarterly for the Southern Management Association from the Department of Management, Texas A&M University.

Scholarly, multidisciplinary articles of empirical research or theory with some focus on the topic as it affects practitioners in general business and public administration. Abstracted in ABI/INFORM, MANAGEMENT CONTENTS. Indexed in the business indexes.

Journal of Police Science and Administration

A quarterly from International Association of Chiefs of Police, Inc.

Abstracted in Criminal Justice Abstracts, NEWSEARCH, Psychological Abstracts, and indexed by the legal indexing services.

Journal of Policy Analysis and Management

A quarterly from Association for Public Policy Analysis and Management. Publisher: John Wiley & Sons, Inc.

This is the successor to *Policy Analysis* and to *Public Policy*. Abstracted in ABI/INFORM, Human Resources Abstracts, Journal of Economic Literature, MANAGEMENT CONTENTS, Sage Urban Studies Abstracts, Social Work Research & Abstracts.

Journal of Public Economics

Published nine times a year from Elsevier Sequoia SA.

Econometric articles. Abstracted in Journal of Economic Literature, Sage Public Administration Abstracts, Sage Urban Studies Abstracts.

Journal of Public Policy and Marketing

A quarterly from the School of Business Administration, University of Michigan.

Articles on business law and public responsibility, on marketing and public administration. Abstracted in ABI/INFORM.

Journal of Research in Crime and Delinquency

A semiannual from Sage Publications, Inc.

Abstracted in Criminal Justice Abstracts, Psychological Abstracts, Sage Urban Studies Abstracts.

Journal of Social Issues

A quarterly from Society for the Psychological Study of Social Issues; published by Plenum Press.

Abstracted in Criminal Justice Abstracts, Educational Administration Abstracts, Psychological Abstracts, Sage Urban Studies Abstracts.

Journal of State Government

A quarterly from the Council of State Governments.

Journal of State Taxation

A quarterly from Panel Publishers.

Abstracted in Legal Resource Index and MANAGE-MENT CONTENTS.

Journal of the American Planning Association

A quarterly from the association.

The journal has a practitioner orientation and many articles deal with careers in planning; but each issue will also contain in-depth articles on general urban planning issues or detailing a specific development.

Abstracted in ABI/INFORM, MANAGEMENT CONTENTS, and U.S. Political Science Documents.

Journal of Urban Affairs

A quarterly from the Division of Environmental and Urban Affairs of Virginia Polytechnic Institute.

Abstracted in Human Resources Abstracts.

Journal of Volunteer Administration

A quarterly from the Association of Volunteer Administration.

Abstracted in Human Relations Abstracts, Sage Public Administration Abstracts.

Land Use and Zoning Digest

A monthly from the American Planning Association.

This is a review of law and zoning legal issues for the professional planner.

Indexed in the legal periodical indexes.

Law and Policy

A quarterly from Baldy Center for Law and Social Policy at State University of New York at Buffalo; published by Sage Publications.

Articles on regulatory activity, social welfare, dispute resolution, economics and criminal justice. Abstracted in Legal Resource Index.

Law and Society Review

A quarterly from Law and Society Association.

Articles on the impact of law, and especially of legal practice, on society. Abstracted in Criminal Justice Abstracts, NEWSEARCH, Psychological Abstracts, Sociological Abstracts, U.S. Political Science Documents, Sage Urban Studies Abstracts, and elsewhere.

Legislative Studies Quarterly

A quarterly from University of Iowa, Comparative Legislative Research Center.

Abstracted in International Political Science Abstracts, U.S. Political Science Abstracts.

Management World

A bimonthly from the American Management Society.

Articles on various aspects of management. Special issues provide valuable information for office management (wordprocessing, telecommunication resources, equipment, etc.).

Abstracted in ABI/INFORM, MANAGEMENT CONTENTS.

M I S (Management Information Service) Report

A monthly from International City Management Association.

Abstracted in Sage Public Administration Abstracts, Urban Affairs Abstracts.

Modern Times

Published ten times a year by Modern Times.

Abstracted in Sage Public Administration Abstracts

Monthly Labor Review

A monthly from the U.S. Bureau of Labor Statistics.

The major publication for current labor statistics including price indexes and work stoppages. Major articles on labor topics and special features relating current labor development add to this journal's value. Abstracted in ABI/INFORM, Economic Literature Index, MANAGEMENT CONTENTS, PROMT, TRADE & INDUSTRY INDEX and the print abstracting services; also covered by all major indexes.

Monthly List of GAO Reports

A monthly from the General Accounting Office.

The list includes abstracts and, thus, provides a way to survey GAO publications.

Nation's Cities Weekly

A tabloid weekly from National League of Cities.

News and feature coverage of federal matters impacting on municipal governments; a special feature tracks the status of legislation in Congress affecting cities. Abstracted in NEWSEARCH, TRADE & INDUSTRY INDEX, Urban Affairs Abstracts.

National Civic Review

A bimonthly from the National Municipal League, Inc.

Focused on local government, this journal includes abstracts and reviews of research into local government topics. Abstracted in Sage Public Administration Abstracts, U.S. Political Science Documents and the legal periodical indexes.

National Contract Management Journal

A quarterly from National Contract Management Association.

Abstracted in ABI/INFORM, MANAGEMENT CONTENTS.

National Journal

A weekly from Government Research Corp.

This covers federal administration politics in a fashion similar to *Congressional Quarterly Weekly Report*: articles, reports, documentation, charts. There is more emphasis on political analysis than in the Congressional Quarterly publications, and less factual or reference content.

National Tax Journal

A quarterly from the National Tax Association, Tax Institute of America.

Reports on research in government finance and taxation, economics and banking. Abstracted in ABI/INFORM, ECONOMIC LITERATURE INDEX, LegalTrac, MANAGEMENT CONTENTS, and TRADE AND INDUSTRY INDEX.

New Directions for Program Evaluation

A quarterly from Evaluation Association.

Articles describe techniques and procedures for evaluation studies. Indexed by the education indexes.

NLC Washington Report to the Nations Cities

Published twice a month by National League of Cities.

Abstracted in Urban Affairs Abstracts

Northwestern University Law Review

A quarterly from Northwestern University, School of Law.

Abstracted in Criminal Justice Abstracts, Sage Public Administration Abstracts and covered by the legal literature indexes.

Parks and Recreation

A monthly from National Recreation and Park Association.

Indexed in MAGAZINE INDEX, P.A.I.S, and other indexes.

Policy Studies Journal

A quarterly from the Policy Studies Organization.

Articles apply the methods of the academic social science disciplines to public policy issues. Abstracted in Human Resource Abstracts, International Political Science Abstracts, Sociological Abstracts and U.S. Political Science Documents.

Policy Studies Review

A quarterly from Policy Studies Organization.

For an academic audience. Abstracted in Educational Administration Abstracts, Human Resources Abstracts, International Political Science Abstracts, Personnel Literature, Sage Public Administration Abstracts, Sociological Abstracts.

Political Science Quarterly

A quarterly from the Academy of Political Science.

This best represents the scholarly discipline of Political Science as practiced by American academics. The journal is also a major book review source. Abstracted in Economic Literature Index, International Political Science Abstracts, Sage Urban Studies Abstracts, U.S. Political Science Documents.

Polity

A quarterly from Northeastern Political Science Association.

Articles for an academic audience. Abstracted in Human Resources Abstracts, International Political Science Abstracts, Sage Public Administration Abstracts, Sage Urban Studies Abstracts, U.S. Political Science Documents.

Public Administration Quarterly

A quarterly from Southern Public Administration Education Foundation. Affiliated with Rider College, Center for Public Policy and Administration.

A scholarly journal with articles on organization behavior, organization development, personnel, and strategic management. Abstracted in ABI/INFORM, MANAGEMENT CONTENTS, Personnel Literature, Sage Public Administration Abstracts, Sage Urban Studies Abstracts.

Public Administration Review

A bimonthly from American Society for Public Administration.

This contains timely, short, scholarly articles on topics of interest in the field of public administration. Abstracted in ABI/INFORM, MANAGEMENT CONTENTS, NEWSEARCH, Sage Public Administration Abstracts, Sage Urban Studies Abstracts, TRADE & INDUSTRY INDEX, U.S. Political Science Documents, and indexed in Social Science Index, Legal Resource Index and others.

Public Budgeting and Finance

A quarterly sponsored by the American Society of Public Administration's Section on Budgeting and Finance.

The sponsor is one of the most active of ASPA's sections. The journal is abstracted in MANAGEMENT CONTENTS, Sage Public Administration Abstracts, Sage Urban Studies Abstracts.

Public Choice

Published nine times a year by the Center for Study of Public Choice, Department of Economics, University of Arizona.

Scholarly articles generally applying economic analysis to issues of banking, consumers affairs and public administration topics. Abstracted in Economic Literature Index, Human Resources Abstracts, Journal of Economic Literature, Sage Public Administration Abstracts, Sage Urban Studies Abstracts, U.S. Political Science Documents.

Public Contract Law Journal

Published three times a year from the American Bar Association, Section on Public Contract Law.

Major law review articles. There is also a newsletter of the Section; it includes brief surveys of recent developments in federal, state and local contract law.

Public Finance Quarterly

A quarterly from Sage Publications, Inc.

Articles on public finance, investment, and financial administration; frequently quantitative analysis and financial modeling. Abstracted in ABI/INFORM, Human Resources Abstracts, Journal of Economic Literature, Sage Urban Studies Abstracts, U.S. POLITICAL SCIENCE DOCUMENTS, and others.

Public Health Reports

A bimonthly from U.S. Public Health Service, Department of Health and Human Services.

Abstracted in Chemical Abstracts, Health Planning and Administration (as well as other health-related services), Human Resources Abstracts.

Public Interest

A quarterly published by National Affairs Inc.

The entire content is not covered by any abstracting service, but this journal of opinion is covered by many indexing services.

Public Management

A monthly from International City Management Association.

This is a practitioner magazine for city and county

managers, mayors and other municipal administrators. Special topic issues have recently treated ethics, police/city manager relations, new technology, affirmative action at city halls. Abstracted in Personnel Literature, Sage Public Administration Abstracts.

Public Personnel Management

A quarterly from International Personnel Management Association.

The major journal covering personnel and managerial topics, business law, office administration and organizational development. Abstracted in ABI/INFORM, Educational Administration Abstracts, Human Relations Abstracts, Personnel Management Abstracts, Personnel Literature, PsycINFO, Psychological Abstracts, Sage Public Administration Abstracts, Work Related Abstracts.

Public Productivity Review

A quarterly from Jossey-Bass, Inc., Publishers.

Productivity studies as well as reviews of related literature. Abstracted in ABI/INFORM, Personnel Literature, Personnel Management Abstracts, Sage Public Administration Abstracts, Sage Urban Studies Abstracts., Urban Affairs Abstracts

Public Roads

A quarterly from U.S. Federal Highway Administration.

Abstracted in INSPEC, PROMT. Indexed in Index to U.S. Government Periodicals.

Public Utilities Fortnightly

Twenty-six issues a year from Public Utilities Reports, Inc., Arlington, VA.

News, articles and special issues on the utilities,

including telecommunications, and finance. Abstracted in Energy Abstracts, Legal Resource Index, MANAGEMENT CONTENTS, TRADE AND INDUSTRY INDEX.

Public Works

A monthly from Public Works Journal Corporation.

Publishes special issues on transportation, roadside maintenance, winter preparedness, water pollution control. Publishes *Public Works Manual*, a special issue on products, services and firms active in public works. Abstracted in INSPEC. Indexed in Applied Science and Technology Index, Engineering Index, TRADE AND INDUSTRY INDEX.

Publius; The Journal of Federalism

A quarterly from the Center for the Study of Federalism.

Scholarly articles by American academics. Abstracted in International Political Science Abstracts, Sage Public Administration Abstracts, Sage Urban Studies Abstracts, Sociological Abstracts.

Review of Public Personnel Administration

Published three times a year; sponsored by the American Society for Public Administration, Section on Personnel Administration and Labor Relations.

Important state by state review articles appear frequently on such topics as merit pay, gender bias, civil service reform. Abstracted in ABI/INFORM, Human Relations Abstracts, Personnel Literature, Personnel Management Abstracts, Sage Urban Studies Abstracts, Urban Affairs Abstracts.

Rural Sociology

A quarterly from Rural Sociological Society.

Abstracted in Abstracts of Health Care Management

Studies, Psychological Abstracts, Sage Urban Studies Abstracts, Sociological Abstracts.

School Law Bulletin (Boston)

A monthly from Quinlan Publishing Co., Inc.

Indexed in Legal Resources Index.

Social Forces

A quarterly from the University of North Carolina Press.

A scholarly sociology journal. Abstracted in Criminal Justice Abstracts, Educational Administration Abstracts, Human Resources Abstracts, Psychological Abstracts, Sage Urban Studies Abstracts, Social Work Research & Abstracts, Sociological Abstracts.

Social Security Bulletin

A monthly from the Social Security Administration.

A major statistical journal covering social security income, public assistance and federal benefit payments.

Social Science Quarterly

From the Southwestern Social Science Association.

The social science journal for an academic audience of most interest to public administrators. Articles regularly deal with social and political issue effecting minorities and the elderly, with issues of elites, volunteerism, privatization and others. Abstracted in all the major abstracting services.

Social Service Review

A quarterly from the School of Social Services Administration, University of Chicago.

Substantial academic articles on all aspects of the social services. Abstracted in Sage Urban Studies Abstracts, Social Work Research and Abstracts, Sociological Abstracts.

Social Work

Published six times a year from the National Association of Social Workers.

Predominantly articles on social work personnel issues with others on social demography and social policy analysis. Abstracted in Criminal Justice Abstracts, Psychological Abstracts, Social Work Research and Abstracts and the health literature indexes.

Socio-Economic Planning Sciences

A bimonthly from Pergamon Press, Inc., Journals Division.

Scholarly articles apply quantitative analysis to social and economic planning issues. Abstracted in Abstracts of Health Care Management Studies and the other medical indexing and abstracting services, Educational Administration Abstracts., Sage Public Administration Abstracts, Sage Urban Studies Abstracts, Sociological Abstracts, and others.

Southern California Law Review

Published six times a year from University of Southern California, Law Center.

A major law review of interest to public administrators. Abstracted in Criminal Justice Abstracts, Sage Public Administration Abstracts, Sage Urban Studies Abstracts and covered by the legal periodical indexes.

State and Local Government Review

Published three times a year from the University of Georgia, Carl Vinson Institute of Government.

Abstracted in Sage Public Administration Abstracts, Sage Urban Studies Abstracts.

State Government News

A monthly from Council of State Governments.

Abstracted in Sage Urban Studies Abstracts.

State Government

A quarterly from Council of State Governments.

Sometimes titled, in bibliographies and elsewhere, *Journal of State Government.* Articles, primarily by academics, on issues affecting the states and case studies of wide applicability. Abstracted in ABI/INFORM, MANAGEMENT CONTENTS, Sage Public Administration Abstracts, and covered by the business periodical indexes.

State Health Reports

Published, along with State Health Notes, ten times a year from the Intergovernmental Health Policy Project.

State Legislatures

Ten times per year from National Conference of State Legislatures.

Articles for state lawmakers and their staffs; the NCSL maintains offices throughout the country and this magazine reports current state developments. Abstracted in Sage Urban Studies Abstracts.

State Policy Reports

*Published six times a year from State Policy
Research, Inc.*

This is a current awareness service reporting on state
government economics and policies.

Survey of Current Business

*A monthly from U.S. Dept. of Commerce, Bureau of
Economic Analysis.*

This valuable monthly regularly publishes data on
public plant and equipment expenditure, state metropolitan and county personal income; it regularly reviews
federal, state and local government fiscal policy. This is
also the single best source of business statistics. It is
widely indexed.

University of Detroit Law Review

*A quarterly from University of Detroit, School of
Law.*

Abstracted in Sage Public Administration Abstracts,
Sage Urban Studies Abstracts and indexed in the legal
periodical indexes.

Urban Affairs Quarterly

From Sage Publications, Inc.

Abstracted in Educational Administration Abstracts,
Human Relations Abstracts, International Political Sci-
ence Abstracts, Sage Public Administration Abstraction,
Sociological Abstracts, U.S. Political Science Documents,
Urban Affairs Abstracts.

Urban and Social Change Review

A semiannual from Boston College, Graduate School of Social Work.

Abstracted in Economic Abstracts, Human Resources Abstracts, Sociological Abstracts, Personnel Management Abstracts, Sage Public Administration Abstracts, Sage Urban Studies Abstracts.

Urban Law and Policy

Published five times a year by Elsevier Science Publishers.

Abstracted in Sage Public Administration Abstracts, Sage Urban Studies Abstracts and indexed in the legal periodical indexes.

Urban Lawyer

A quarterly from American Bar Association, Urban, State and Local Government Law Section.

An important national journal on urban law. Abstracted in Sage Public Administration Abstracts, Sage Urban Studies Abstracts, and covered by the legal indexing services.

Washington Monthly

Published eleven times a year by Washington Monthly Co.

Investigative journalism on the function and impact of the Washington, DC bureaucracy. This magazine is indexed by the major newspaper and online indexing services.

Washington University Journal of Urban and Contemporary Law

Published twice a year.

Abstracted in Human Resources Abstracts and covered by the legal periodical indexes.

Ways & Means

A quarterly from National Center for Policy Alternatives.

Reports on innovative developments in state and local government. Abstracted in Urban Affairs Abstracts.

Work and Occupations

A quarterly from Sage Publications, Inc.

Abstracted in Personnel Literature, Psychological Abstracts, Sage Public Administration Abstracts.

Yale Journal on Regulation

A semiannual from Yale University School of Law, Yale Journal on Regulation Staff.

Indexed by the legal periodical and the health care indexing services.

IV. DIRECTORIES OF PERIODICALS

Magazines for Libraries

6th ed. New York: R.R. Bowker, 1989.

Although not a directory, this is a valuable source of information about 6,500 periodicals which over 100 consultants in special fields consider to be basic to their field. The annotations, by Bill and Linda Sternberg Katz, the editors, are often evaluative. The work is not organized for identifying public administration periodicals, but the user can be confident of finding a useful annotation on most individual titles searched.

Ulrich's International Periodical Directory 1989-90

28th ed. New York: R.R. Bowker, 1989.

This is the major directory. It is indispensable for libraries, where it may be consulted. The directory is available online through Dialog; however, in the past, we have found the print service more up to date.

National Directory of Newsletters and Reporting Services

3rd ed. Detroit, MI: Gale Research Co., 1987.

Using this directory of newsletters, we created a list of nearly 300 newsletters and print services relevant to public administration. We were not able to look at most of them and do not mention them in this *Desk Book*; however, a reader building a specialized public administration library should look at this directory.

Part 5
ONLINE AND OTHER MACHINE BASED SERVICES

This part of the *Desk Book* will answer questions about this important method of obtaining public administration information and other non-paper services. It is not a list of online databases relevant to Public Administration. Those have been cited throughout where the equivalent paper copy is cited or under the appropriate subject. Part 5 is divided as follows:

    I. An introduction and overview of online services.

    II. Suggestions for users of these services.

    III. Description of major providers of database services.

IV. Description of databases not described elsewhere in this guide.

V. Description of CD-ROM and other machine-readable data.

VI. Sources of further information.

We have included some approximation-of-cost information since, unlike most library services, there is usually a fee for online service based on the cost to the library. We have also included information on how to keep up-to-date including the phone numbers for online service providers. New vendors, online databases and other machine-readable products are rapidly developing and are actively marketed. Often the most current information is to be obtained only from vendors and other direct sources.

I. INTRODUCTION

What is meant by online services is an access to machine-readable data files through use of data transmission phone lines. Most often an intermediary service, a database vendor such as Dialog Information Service, acts for the user by providing a supermarket of databases from which to choose. The vendors provide one billing process for all costs (phone line charges, database royalties, surcharges for time spent searching and for records downloaded) and a single set of commands for searching all databases. They also provide the training, inexpensive practice databases and specialized manuals necessary to use online services effectively.

The usual chain of events is this: (1) You or a librarian or information specialist with a computer terminal and phone transmission modem place a call to the local number of one of the data transmission phone services (such as Telenet); (2) once connected, the terminal is "online" and is used to call one of the database vendors or retailers with whom you have a contract; you provide your password for access and billing purposes; (3) once logged on with the vendor, you specify what database or file is to be searched; (4) through the vendor's software you use keyboard commands to search the specific machine-readable file of data (which may consist of population statistics, citations to journal articles, descriptions of associations or whatever); (5) with your search complete you may sort the results in a variety of ways and order your selected records displayed in whole or in part at the terminal, printed out on a printer or downloaded to a floppy disk.

Much of this process can be automated. A librarian or information specialist can provide a client with citations to and summaries of a dozen current articles on privatization of government auditing and assessing services in three to five minutes. They can supply the name, address and phone number of the larger firms in your region that supply, for instance, bar code printers or snow removal tractors in about the same time. The cost, in these illustrations, is under $20. The online industry has flourished, reaching many more users than the earlier "time sharing" and "batch" use of data tapes, primarily because of the services of the database vendors such a Dialog Information Services, the intermediary. They simplify access, provide an economical "pay only for what you receive" charge, and give uniform access to the many, varied collections of information on magnetic tapes presently available.

If you are considering the addition of online services to your present information resources, we advise contracting with Dialog for their services, literature and initial training. Expand on the basis of that experience. Information and information technology are marketed enthusiastically and this is not a settled industry; hence, some experience with the largest and most successful vendor is a valuable basis for later decisions.

II. RECOMMENDATIONS

The modern horn of plenty of information has created a condition where the end user of online information services either must discuss their needs in detail with an information specialist or must apply themselves seriously to learning information gathering methods, including online searching.

The information needs of a public administration practitioner, researcher or student are often not as clearly defined, as precise and specific, as those of someone in science or medicine. An online search for literature on the toxic effects of a specific, relatively rare chemical compound will retrieve all or most of that literature. This is not true in the area of urban planning, public employee productivity, the management of a bureau, etc. This does not mean that online literature searches are not useful; they can be the most thorough, efficient and economical way to find out what you need to know. But it does mean that those performing the search, usually a librarian, must have as much information about your needs as possible. Online searching does not encourage browsing or serendipity. Use print services for that, or use machine-based in-house library services.

The professional business information services (such as *ABI/INFORM*) include all major public administration periodicals and include summaries of articles. Also, *Psychological Abstracts* (PsychINFO online) covers most periodical literature dealing with public administration management, personnel, occupational and public opinion issues. The professional legal information sources are very rich in U.S. public administration topics.

III. DATABASE VENDORS

Most individual database searches are conducted through the intermediary service of a retailer or vendor of databases such as BRS or Dialog Information Services. These vendors provide access to many separately named databases. This section is provided because of the important role of the vendor. The phone numbers can be used to secure current, introductory literature and contract information from the vendors.

BRS Information Technologies. (800)345-4277.

A small annual password fee opens access to BRS's 140 files. Searching is "Pay As You Go" with per hour charges from $15 to $125 plus surcharges for each record printed according to format. Telecommunication charges add $8-$14 per hour. A set of "AidPages" (one page guides to each database giving the fields in each record and other details) and a manual are inexpensive and are necessary.

The full text of articles from most indexed periodicals may be ordered online and are supplied within 48 hours. BRS also offers reduced-rate searching designed for individual end-users who contract with them.

CompuServe. (800)848-8990.

This menu-driven online service is designed for the individual personal computer user, not the librarian or information specialist. It consists primarily of access to special interest bulletin boards or "Forums" and consumer-oriented services (news, weather, travel, electronic shopping, games) along with business information databases. However, it also includes a number of public affairs and demographic databases: 1980 Census data, a Social Security database, demographics by Zip code, county profiles, an index of GPO publications with automated ordering, a directory of federal officials, *Rehabilitation Research* database, and others. There is a small start-up fee, inexpensive manuals and a day-time $12.50

per hour or evening $6 per hour cost which is payable by credit card.

Dialog Information Services. (800)334-2564.

A major online service since the early 1970's, Dialog now provides access to more than 380 databases. As well as handling a large number of databases, Dialog provides excellent documentation and frequent training programs for searchers. Documentation on the databases and on searching methods (including the necessary "Bluesheet" search aids) and full-day initial and special searcher training (available frequently in major cities) will cost about two hundred dollars. Per-hour charges are $15 to $150, depending on the database. Some business information databases have substantial added charges for each full record downloaded.

In most circumstances, a user will be able to identify certain databases that fit their needs. Once they have searched these databases a few times, they can arrive at accurate cost estimates for this type of information resource. For many special libraries online searches and article delivery ordered online are a cost-effective alternative to subscription and storage of paper periodicals.

Dialog also offers reduced-rate services designed for end-users who contract with them.

EasyNet. (800)841-9553.

From Telebase Systems, Inc., this is a "gateway" service which provides an interface between the end user (rather than trained searchers) and the database vendors such as BRS, Data-Star, Dialog, H.W. Wilson, NewsNet, VU/TEXT, and others. A common command language, a single billing and certain "network" facilities are the added value of this and similar services. In other words, another middleman, one which occasional users of multiple vendors will find they do not resent.

Information Access Company (IAC). (800)227-8431.

Although IAC is vendor only of their own information

products, they are an early and successful provider of library information services employing new technology. Their indexes to business periodicals (more than 800 and including local business press, public administration periodicals, trade newspapers and the academic journals), to popular magazines, law periodicals and the major national newspapers are to be found in many libraries. The indexes have been available on microfiche, they have run on 16mm film readers and at computer terminals attached to 12 inch laser optic disks and, now, CD-ROM players. IAC databases have been long available online through Dialog and other services.

IAC products (*LEGAL RESOURCE INDEX, MAGAZINE INDEX, MANAGEMENT CONTENTS, NATIONAL NEWSPAPER INDEX* and *NEWSEARCH, TRADE & INDUSTRY INDEX* and others) provide subject indexing, with the online and CD-ROM products searchable on any field of the citation-like record. There are generally no abstracts.

Mead Data Central. (800)346-9759.

Mead Data created *LEXIS*, the full text online legal search service in 1973. Until recently (see *WESTLAW*) they had no competitor and are still the leading provider of this type of law information service. In the early 1980's they developed *NEXIS* to provides full text online general and business periodical and news services. Their database access is organized into groups called libraries and they do not correspond as directly to print services as do those available through Dialog. Consequently, although they are a major provider, you will not find them cited as frequently in this *Desk Book.*

Whereas using Dialog services mainly consists of searching bibliographic citation, abstract, directory or numeric files, Mead Data's services mainly consists of searching the full text of a select set of publications. Like Dialog, Mead Data is constantly expanding its offerings.

NEXIS includes the major wire services, over 200 newspapers, newsletters and regional business magazines, more than 280 selected business and general circulation magazines and journals, special libraries of professional accounting documents (produced in conjunction with the American Institute of Certified Public Accountants) and groups of trade, technology and finance publications.

They provide training for searchers, which is essential. Online and display charges are comparable to those of Dialog and other vendors; that is, typical searches (other than the very quick) will cost $30 or more.

NewsNet. (800)345-1301.

A large number of specialized newsletters are made available through this online vendor including several federal contracts, utilities, consumer, communications, small business, environment and Federal Trade Commission watch newsletters. Groups of newletters can be searched at once and full-text is available online at costs similar to *NEXIS* full-text services.

VU/TEXT. (800)258-8080.

VU/TEXT is the major provider of regional newspaper databases online (38 at current count) as well as of an increasing number of other news services, full text periodicals and other publications. As with other vendors of full text material, careful attention must be paid to search strategy; the number of surprising (and irrelevant) occurrences of words and relations between words that occur in massive collections of full text is truly impressive. VU/TEXT prints the first paragraph of each record as part of its basic citation and it provides for locating your search terms in the context of the full text as well as other methods of limiting the amount of output you have to scan for material relevant to your needs.

Recent enhancements allow you to search all newspapers in 1988 or 1987 with the same search. They are increasing their coverage of all types of news media. Pricing is similar to that established by Dialog but most users find actual costs higher because of the combination of awkward searching software and full text.

West Publishing Company. (800)328-9352.

West is the major publisher of legal material. Their online service, *WESTLAW*, incorporates the case law material in the National Reporter System, the *United States Code, Shepard's Citations*, a tax and many other specialized law libraries. The West system of topics and key numbers and their headnotes and digests are a very well established feature of legal research and this online service employs them.

As with *LEXIS* this service is available either on a contract basis for unlimited use (searching and downloading) though specialized data transmission phone lines or on a pay-as-you-go basis with a personal computer and modem. *WESTLAW* includes a gateway to VU/TEXT's databases and to Dialog.

H.W. Wilson Company. (800)367-6770.

This firm has been the major provider of print periodical subject indexes to libraries. Their online service, *WILSONLINE*, corresponds to the recent years of their print services. Each record is a citation to a periodical article and, as with all the bibliographic databases, each field (author, title, subject, journal, etc.) may be searched. Only their *Book Review Digest* includes summaries along with the bibliographic citations.

The Wilson paper indexes can be found in most libraries and several of them (*Bibliographic Index, Biography Index, Book Review Digest, General Science Index*) provide unique popular services. However, as a vendor of databases H.W. Wilson Company is a mom and pop store rather than a supermarket.

Some of their indexing is also available as CD-ROM products.

IV. ADDITIONAL DATABASES OF SPECIAL INTEREST IN PUBLIC ADMINISTRATION

Machine-readable data files of interest to public administrators are described throughout this *Desk Book* and, in the SUBJECT INDEX, are cited under many subjects. Those described here are rather specialized and do not appear in other Parts of the *Desk Book.*

A. DEMOGRAPHIC DATA

CENDATA

This database began online in 1984 and presents select Bureau of the Census information. It is updated daily. *CENDATA* contains both press releases and numeric data excerpted from economic and demographic reports, mainly summary statistics. Older material is removed as new material is entered.

The Bureau of Census and other federal data-generating agencies do not compete with the private value-added suppliers of census and other demographic data. Thus, easily accessible and easily manipulatable databases from the government are, like this one, limited to excerpts and summary data. *CENDATA* is available online from Dialog.

DONNELLEY DEMOGRAPHICS

From Donnelley Marketing Services the records in this file contain the 1980 census data, current-year estimates and five-year projections and proprietary estimates and projections for states, counties, cities, towns, ZIP areas and for age, sex, race, industry, occupation, martial status, family size, education, housing, income, etc. Only user selected elements are reported and format is highly variable. With some experience, it provides a quick way to download specific data elements. The file is available through Dialog.

This is only one of a number of demographic data files which present U.S. Bureau of Census and Bureau of Economic Analysis data and add value to it with updating estimates, forecast data and by supplementing it with less familiar public data (Internal Revenue Service data, public utility data, etc.). Developers, retailers and marketing services are the primary clients of these data services which, consequently, specialize in information for small geographic areas (that is, markets). Often data of most use to a public administrator is also small area data. Users should thoroughly investigate competing products (including those mentioned below from CACI, Inc., and from Urban Systems Research and Engineering, Inc.) since quite different value-added approaches are used by each firm.

HRIN

Human Resource Information Network from Executive Telecom Systems, Inc. (a BNA subsidiary) is an online service through the producer which accesses BNA's massive employment and labor relations information base. Also included are news services for personnel managers, business and social science databases (such as *ABI/IN-FORM* and *PsycINFO*), data files on employment demographics, occupational profiles, pay and salary surveys, seminar and training programs and other topics. It is intended as a single point of online access for personnel practitioners. Cost and complexity is less than that involved in searching BNA (or the CCH or Prentice-Hall) labor relations online reporter services.

SITE II

Produced by CACI, Inc., the major commercial demographic data source, this database contains historical and forecast demographic data for any area, of any size or shape, in the United States, based upon the census of population and housing, current year estimates and five-year projections. Areas can be defined by specifying latitude and longitude or by using any combination of states, counties, cities, Metropolitan Statistical Areas and components, ZIP code areas, census tracts, etc. Data is available for the 1970 and 1980 Census of Population and Housing, and includes population, housing characteristics, households, occupation, income distribution, educational attainment, age distribution, utilities profile, race distribution and automobile ownership.

Along with CACI, I.P. Sharp Associates is also a major provider of demographic data, including that produced by the National Planning Data Corporation.

X/REGION (Regional Economic Data Base)

This is from Urban Systems Research and Engineering, Inc., (202) 293-3240, and provides historical and forecasted annual economic data by Metropolitan Statistical Areas, State and the U.S. as a whole. Regional data is available for over 100 industrial sectors (Standard Industrial Classification groupings) on: domestic output; payrolls; employment; personal consumption expenditures; and equipment investment. In addition, *X/REGION* contains regional data on: types of income; population, deaths and births; labor force and unemployment statistics; construction expenditures by type; federal government expenditures by function and total state and local government expenditures.

B. FEDERAL GOVERNMENT ACTIVITIES AND PUBLICATIONS

CIS/INDEX

From Congressional Information Service, Inc., available through Dialog and others. CIS also produces the principle indexing of governmental statistics, this database corresponds to their monthly print index to congressional publications and public laws. Covering from 1970 to the present with general subject, witness, author, geographic, committee name, Bill or Report number and other indexing, it includes descriptive abstracts to the whole and separate parts of documents and prices and call numbers necessary to find the documents in a depository library or in CIS's corresponding microform service. Thus, this services covers every significant publication issued by nearly 300 House, Senate and Joint Committees and Subcommittees of Congress.

CONGRESSIONAL RECORD ABSTRACTS

This database is produced by the National Standards Association (Bethesda, MD) and available from Dialog and others. It covers from 1976 to the present. It provides comprehensive coverage of the *Congressional Record*, the official journal of proceedings of the United States Congress and contains references to: bills and resolutions, amendments to bills and resolutions, committee and subcommittee reports, legislation recently signed into law, floor actions, schedules of committee, speeches, participation in debates and inserted materials by members of Congress.

FEDERAL REGISTER ABSTRACTS

This database is available through Dialog and others. It provides comprehensive coverage of the *Federal Register*, which is to say, of the regulatory agencies' regulations, rules, proposed rules, legal notices, meetings and hearings, and also of presidential proclamations, Executive Orders, Notices and notices of rules taking effect each day. It is of particular interest to those involved with regulation and compliance requirements.

GPO MONTHLY CATALOG

This is the online equivalent of the print *Monthly Catalog of United States Government Publications* from 1976 to the present. Unlike the print service, it is searchable online by any word or indexing number in the record; however, the abstracts in the Monthly Catalog are usually confined to bibliographic formalities. Although far superior to the print service, this online file does not reward common subject searching in the way the CIS products do.

It is available from BRS and Dialog and information provided usually indicates the price, the document's library call number and ordering information. Government Printing Office material currently in print and available for purchase from the GPO and GPO bookstores can be search in a companion database *GPO PUBLICATIONS REFERENCE FILE.*

ICPERS (Instant Computer Public Employment Relations Search).

This online service, along with the Federal Employment Decision Search, is produced by Labor Relations Press. Together, they are the online form of the National Public Employment Reporter, Federal Labor Relations Reporter, Federal Merit System Reporter and Labor Arbitration Information System. The databases contain all decisions of every public sector labor relations board and commission, as well as all related court decisions issued nation-wide each year and related material. A user would need to be familiar with the print services and its Key numbering system and indexing.

It is available online from Labor Relations Press and not through an online database vendor.

INDEX TO U.S. GOVERNMENT PERIODICALS

This database covers 185 periodicals produced by over 100 U.S. federal agencies from 1980 forward. There are no abstracts; author, title and assigned subject headings may be searched. The more familiar government magazines (*Monthly Labor Review, Federal Reserve Bulletin*, etc.) are covered by other online indexes but many magazines are covered only by this service. There is a corresponding print index published by the information supplier, Infordata International, Inc.

The database is available as part of WILSONLINE.

C. LAW SERVICES

LABORLAW

This is a monthly updated online product of The Bureau of National Affairs, Inc. (BNA) and corresponds to their comprehensive labor relations looseleaf reporter services (See Reporter Services). It does not include the full text of subject cases as do the print services. Thus, LABORLAW is a guide to the decisions of federal and state courts, administrative bodies and arbitrators in the subject areas of labor/management relations, fair employment practices, labor arbitration awards, wages and hours, employee benefits and occupational safety and health.

It is available from BNA and as a "library" within the LEXIS and WESTLAW services.

LEXIS

Mead Data Central, and affiliated information suppliers, provide this database of case law material. It is an extensive professional service designed for law firms, law libraries and schools, accounting firms and others. *LEXIS* contains Federal and State court reported cases, Federal and State constitutions, codes, rules and regulations, decisions from certain government agencies and other legal material. There are comprehensive patent, trademark, copyright law, securities, tax, labor libraries and others. The library of state materials includes the case law of all 50 states and DC. *LEXIS* also incorporates online many information products of the publishers Matthew Bender, Shepards and BNA (see Part VI of this Desk Book on legal reporter services).

Generally, this is a tool not used or accessible outside of law schools and the legal and accounting professions.

WESTLAW

From West Publishing Company, a major publisher of legal material, this incorporates the case law material in the National Reporter System, the US Code, Shepard's Citations, and tax as well as specialized law libraries. The

West system of topics and key numbers and their head-notes and digests are very well established feature of legal research and this online service employs these.

As with *LEXIS* this service is available either on a contract basis for unlimited use (searching and downloading) though specialized data transmission phone lines or on a pay-as-you-go basis with a PC and PC modem.

D. NEWS DATABASES

NEWSEARCH

This is a valuable index of citations to the current issues of 400 periodicals (from the file MAGAZINE INDEX), the five major national newspapers (from the file National Newspaper Index), the current issues of 500 academic and trade journals (from the file MANAGEMENT CONTENTS) and those journals and newspaper in the LEGAL RE-SOURCE INDEX. This file contains only citations to articles in this literature but it provides very quick articles on topics of general interest (news, biographical pieces, products, companies and social issues in the news).

It, and the companion files, are available from BRS, Dialog and Mead Data Central's *LEXIS/NEXIS*. They are produced by Information Access Corp.

UPI NEWS

One of the several daily updated newswire services available through Dialog, Mead Data Central, NewsNet and other vendors. As a newswire service it is not a consistent source of information for past news. For that search the various full text newspaper databases available through VU/TEXT where news of recently past events corresponds more consistently to the printed papers which are themselves usually available on microfilm in local public libraries.

The United Press International wire database includes both news and the UPI columns and standing features.

V. CD-ROM AND OTHER NON-ONLINE SOURCES OF MACHINE READABLE INFORMATION

A. ON CD-ROM

1. Introduction

The advent of the standardized large capacity compact disks (with about five times the data storage capacity of the largest readily available harddisks for personal computers) has introduced extensive marketing of indexing and numeric data files in CD-ROM format. By adding a CD-ROM drive (at about the cost of a large personal computer harddisk) and purchasing through subscription your data or indexing on CD-ROM, you can access an indexing or statistical database without telecommunication or online vendor charges. The advantage of unlimited cost-free searching and downloading (within the context of your prepaid subscription) is very great for a constantly used indexing database. These products will soon be in all public and university libraries.

CD-ROM disks (Compact Disk-Read Only Memory) are stable, unchangeable, small and almost indestructible: an ideal medium for compressed storage of large sets of numeric data, reference volumes, encyclopedias, massive dictionaries, etc. As yet there is no price advantage for the consumer of this form of information; however, wiser heads may prevail. Whether high priced and slowly, or lower priced and rapidly, CD-ROM will become a major information medium. Interested parties in the U.S. Bureau of Census expect CD-ROM to become the information storage medium of the future and to replace "miles upon miles" of shelf space. One CD-ROM stores the equivalent of 275,000 pages of information (about 200 pounds of paper). The Bureau will release all 1990 census material (all that is available on magnetic tape) on CD-ROM.

The Bureau issued its first CD-ROM in 1988, the 1980 census data (income, education, etc., by ZIP code), previously only available on four magnetic tapes (the equivalent of 1,600 floppy disks). Their second CD-ROM provides the 1982 census of retail trade and agriculture by ZIP code. The Bureau plans to release all 1987 Economic Censuses that will be available on magnetic tape also on laser disks. They plan to include retrieval software and make the file formats compatible with major microcomputer database software.

The manufacturing cost advantage which the CD-ROM industry gains by piggy-backing on the music recording industry's compact disks is significant. However, costs remain high, much higher in most cases than the print equivalents and high enough to make the timely, faster and pay-only-for-what-you-use features of online services attractive. Federal public domain data on CD-ROM is available for $35 to $450 per database; value added statistics and indexing/abstracting annual subscriptions are from $500 to over $5000 per year.

Libraries with a steady flow of patrons who might otherwise wish to use online services or special libraries, agencies, or information centers with a high level of use of specific databases, will find CD-ROM a cost-efficient way to supply information. Since CD-ROM products are intended for direct patron use, without the intervention of a trained searcher, they are usually provided with menu-driven searching method and with on-screen help.

CD-ROM players and disk formats are standardized and, assuming the use of industry standard IBM PC or compatible machines, the selection of hardware is not a problem. Searching software is still highly variable; however, since software is usually provided with the disk data, the public administrator can concentrate on discovering what information they want to buy in this format asking themselves how frequently this data is sought. This process is being aided by the emergence of retailers, vendors, of CD-ROM products and CD-ROM database subscriptions.

Concerning this medium of information especially, use only very current information. Phone queries and product catalogs are the most current information.

2. Some CD-ROM Products and Vendors

Abt Electronic Library. (617)661-1300.

They distribute SilverPlatter and 30 or so additional titles and plan special CD-ROM products of considerable interest to public administrators. One of the first is a very large collection of criminal justice literature and data on one disk.

R.R. Bowker. (212)645-9700.

Provides *Books in Print, Ulrich's International Periodicals Directory* and other tools on CD-ROM at around twice the cost of the multi-volume print sets.

The Faxon Company. (617)329-3350.

A major periodical jobber used by information centers who subscribe to many journals and magazines and who wish to have their subscriptions processed collectively, Faxon now handles CD-ROM product subscriptions also.

Hopkins Technology. (612)931-9376.

A new vendor of data from Department of Commerce and other data tapes on CD-ROM. The inexpensive disks include consumer price index, 1913-1988 for 50 areas, industial production index, export/import price index, interest rates (90 types, 1925-1988) and other time series.

Meridian Data, Inc. (408)438-3100.

A new vendor of CD-ROM hardware, including networks and, through other vendors, of databases. Increasingly, like this firm, compatibility with Ethernet, Novell and other networking products and multiple-disk, multiple-user products are being supported.

Microsoft Corp. (206)882-8080.

As an indication of things-to-come in this information format, there is *Microsoft Bookshelf: CD ROM Refer-*

ence Library with the CD containing a standard dictionary, *Roget's Thesaurus*, the 1987 *World Almanac and Book of Facts*, *Bartlett's Familiar Quotations*, the ZIP code directory, Lorna Daniells's *Business Information Sources* and other tools.

SilverPlatter Information, Inc. (617)239-0306.

A major provider of subscription to many CD-ROM databases. They provide hardware and uniform searching software for each database and with their software the files are searchable by any content in the record and complex searches (using "and," "or," "not" and proximity of words). Silver-Platter also provides multi-user products employing Ethernet cards and multiple disk players and the necessary software.

University Microfilms International (UMI). (800)521-3044, ext 234.

A number of indexing and other CD-ROM products are available from this national dissertation, periodical and microfilming center.

SilverPlatter and UMI certainly would be firms to contact for those considering adding CD-ROM information products. UMI's *NEWSPAPER ABSTRACTS* on CD-ROM is not identical to UMI's *NEWSPAPER ABSTRACTS* online from Dialog; this is usual with CD-ROM products.

3. Sources of Information

Optical Publishing Directory

3rd ed. Medford, NJ: Learned Information, Inc., 1988.

The previous edition of this service listed 84 optical storage media titles (where the text or data is permanently etched on disks and read by means of laser optics). This edition lists nearly 200 . It provides one page profiles of products and sections on vendors, CD-ROM services and hardware.

Meckler Corporation. (203)226-6967.

The publisher of *CD-ROMs in Print*, an annual and several periodicals for this industry and CD-ROM product users.

B. DATA ON DISKETTES

Publishers and other information suppliers continue to experiment with marketing information on microcomputer floppy disks. This has been a favored way of supplying updates to software and it also fits certain forms of data distribution.

Following are some of the products available on this medium:

CD-ROM; An Annotated Bibliography

Englewood, CO: Libraries Unlimited, 1988.

Available on IBM, MacIntosh and Apple disk formats at about the cost of a printed volume. Also available in print, 150 pages long. The information is through 1987.

Conference Board, CBDB Data Disk

Monthly from Conference Board.

A substantial collection of economic time series created and updated through subscription by the Conference Board. A spreadsheet type of retrieval software is provided with subscriptions.

County and City Data Book Data Disk

Washington, DC: U.S. Bureau of Census, 1988.

Available on standard IBM PC disks from the Bureau. The data is keyed to the printed edition and, unlike the 1983 floppy disk edition, identifying names are linked to data and the file easily manipulated with spreadsheet or the newer wordprocessing software. The Advisory Commission on Intergovernmental Relations also makes Bureau of Census data available on diskettes, e.g., *County and City Finance Data on Microcomputer Diskettes* which includes expenditure and debt data for state and local governments.

BLS Data Diskettes

Irregular from U.S. Bureau of Labor Statistics.

The Bureau's series of data are available on standard diskettes at $35 each or with annual subscriptions. The series now includes consumer expenditure surveys, CPI and other standard price index data, economic growth projections and historical time series, employment cost index. hours, earnings and other labor force data including productivity data and occupational injury rate data. Annual subscriptions vary from $288 for CPI to $58 for shorter sets.

C. MAGNETIC TAPES

Public Administrators using data on one of the industry standard formats of magnetic tape will usually have encountered it as a service of their organization's data processing center, that is, data running on mainframes or minicomputers and available on dumb terminals at appropriate locations. Personnel, payroll, demographic, enrollment and other data regularly used by the bureau or institution usually arrives to the end user from this source. Such information is not usually sought, or available, to satisfy an individual's unique information requirements.

The following are sources of information on this medium that might be particularly relevant to the public administrator.

Federal Statistical Data Bases

Annual from Oryx Press.

This is the successor to the U.S. National Technical Information Services's *Directory of Computerized Data Files*. It is of interest primarily to those using databases on mainframe computers.

Census Catalog and Guide

Annual from U.S. Department of Commerce, Bureau of the Census.

This is the most user friendly of the Bureau's publications. It describes the statistical series and other information products including online and data tape, optical disk and diskette products. An appendix provides "sources of assistance," both Washington and local offices. This publication also reproduces especially useful issues of the newsletter *Factfinder for the Nation* which explain various products and their schedule of publication. Standard format magnetic tape of data series from the Bureau are available at about $70 per tape.

Guide to Resources and Services

Irregular from Inter-University Consortium for Political and Social Research.

The consortium is a partnership between the Center for Political Studies, Institute for Social Research, University of Michigan and several hundred universities. It makes available to members data tapes of demographic data, election statistics, public opinion, health and others.

State Data Centers

These are listed in an appendix to the above Census Catalog and Guide.

These came into being primarily to further public access to Bureau of Census data. Several we know of actually do that and additionally produce valuable information products.

An Inventory of Data Sources for Governmental and Other Nonprofit Organizations

A pamphlet from the Data Availability Subcommittee, Government and Nonprofit Section Research Committee, American Accounting Association, February, 1985.

Although out of date, this was a well-prepared forty page inventory of state, university and association data files.

VI. DIRECTORIES AND OTHER SOURCES OF INFORMATION

Database Directory

4th ed. Knowledge Industry, 1988.

A print directory produced from the online counterpart and updated with a monthly *Database Alert.* The coverage is similar to the directories below; this one provides somewhat more information on each database.

DataPro Directory of On-Line Services

Delran, NJ: Datapro Research Corporation, 1982-

A two volume loose-leaf service from this major computer industry information provider. Included are sketches of more than 200 remote computing service providers, material on the online industry and online services and brief sketches of over 4,000 available databases. It is the most comprehensive, and most expensive, tool listed here, but major libraries with active online services will have it available.

Directory of Online Databases

4th ed. New York: Cuadra/Elsevier, 1988.

This directory is also available online through through WESTLAW, CompuServe and other services.

DATABASE OF DATABASES

Urbana, IL: M.E. Williams, Inc. and Information Retrieval Research Lab., University of Illinois at Urbana-Champaign, 1985-

This online file is available from Dialog and corresponds to the 2 vol. *Computer-Readable Databases* (Chicago: American Library Association, 1985). The online directory has not been updated. As with the online file of the item above, online searching by names, descriptions and assigned "descriptors" (indexed terms) makes possible more complete recovery of information than the necessarily general alphabetic indexing of the print volumes.

Encyclopedia of Information Systems and Services

8th ed. Detroit, MI: Gale Research Company, 1988.

This guide includes entries which list and describe the organizations, systems and services involved in the electronic information industry. These include databases and their producers, online vendors, gateways and networks developed for information transmission, database creators, library networks, commercial firms specializing in information retrieval and the consultants, associations, research agencies and publishers associated with the industry. Also included in the coverage are offline files available on magnetic tape, diskette or CD-ROM and other optical technologies, as well as online in realtime databases.

Manual of Online Search Strategies

Boston, MA: G.K. Hall, 1988.

Separately authored chapters covers the online databases available in major subject areas. The chapters on the social and behavioral sciences, law and business and economics are of most relevance.

Online Database Search Services Directory

2nd ed. Detroit, MI: Gale Research Company, 1988.

This is a guidebook intended to assist users in finding local online search services. It is arranged by state and then city and then by service provider. Entries include address and telephone number, contact person, staff size, services provided and fee policy. Entries include libraries as well as for profit information consultants and firms.

Online Review

A bimonthly from Learned Information, Inc.

A journal of news, case-study and research articles and brief reviews. This and the following journal serve information professionals primarily. Annually it reviews online directories.

Online

A bimonthly from Online, Inc.

A monthly journal which along with a companion monthly *Database* provides valuable review articles on online services and databases.

Part 6
LAW AND REGULATORY REPORTER SERVICES

Because this part of the *Desk Book* deals with a type of information service more likely to be found in a professional law library, rather than in a university or public library, we have included an introduction to this type of material and an introduction to law libraries. This is followed by a selection of law and regulatory reporter services which the public administration researcher or practitioner may find useful. With each title we indicate the publisher and the call number, and the library location number, by which the title can be found in most law libraries. Finally, there is a list of the major publisher's full name and a contact number.

I. REPORTER SERVICES AND THEIR USES: INTRODUCTION

Several publishers produce services for the law and accounting professions which are of considerable value to public administrators. These are known as "reporter services" (for their primary role of immediately reporting legislative, administrative and judicial developments in special areas) or "loose-leaf services" (for their published form in post or ring binders). Bureau of National Affairs (BNA), Commerce Clearing House (CCH), and Prentice Hall (P-H) are major publishers. The services are expensive (average cost in 1987 was $659) and owe their success to the fact that administrative, judicial and legislative raw information publications from governmental sources are difficult to access, inadequately indexed or do not exist.

The advantages of reporter services for the public administration practitioner are their timeliness (in advance of available "official" published sources), their unity (each service devoted to a particular subject which it indexes extensively), and their inclusion of valuable non-legal information. For example, labor relations reporters will include comprehensive arrays of the most current and historical Consumer Price Index data and will report on labor relations trends and may provide contract clause-finders and contract excerpts. State-specific reporters on taxation provide full text of statutes, as well as court decisions, rulings and interpretations. Many reporters provide explanatory discussion, glossaries and bibliographies. Some include reports of surveys, assemble and reprint key articles, provide encyclopedia-like introductory essays, survey current trends, theories, etc.

Because these services are sometimes valuable for the public administrator, and because they are usually regarded as the provenance of law libraries, a fairly extensive treatment is provided here. Following each title we indicate the publisher and the full names of the publishers and their phone numbers (for current catalogs and prices) appear at the end of this part of the *Desk Book.*

II. LAW LIBRARIES: INTRODUCTION

Law libraries, typically, do not restrict access to their reference, public document or periodical collections. However, they are not organized as service-oriented public or university libraries but rather as "special libraries" serving a trained, professional clientele. We strongly advise you not to expect law library staff (who are organized to maintain their special materials and serve a clientele trained in the use of law libraries) to deal with phone querys, to provide staff to locate material for you or explain its uses or to answer questions which professional legal training would answer. You will find that most loose-leaf services contain a "How to Use" introductory section. The use of a guide such as Edward J. Bander, *Searching the Law* (1987), which is subject organized and explanatory rather than merely descriptive, is also beneficial. Again, your habits of use in a state, public or university library do not carry over into law libraries.

With respect to online services, major law libraries provide access to LEXIS and WESTLAW for trained searchers. Law students routinely receive such training. They do not offer online access as a public service. Much of the content of the paper looseleaf services described below are available to trained searchers in online form.

With the titles below you will find a Call Number (a locator within the library's organized collection, such as [KF 3576]). You may use the Call Numbers, which originate with the Library of Congress, to locate reporter services within the rational organization of any law library. These services can also be located by title through the card catalog of a law library. You may also find a Union List of such services in the region in your own university or professional library (for example, *New England Law Library Consortium Union List of Loose Leaf Services*). Also, national online cataloging services enable librarians to locate holdings of a service if you know the exact title.

The following annual publication lists all such services in

print and is subject indexed: *Legal Looseleafs in Print*, Teaneck, NJ: Infosources, 1988.

Two loose-leaf reporter services deserve special notice. They can be found in most library reference collections.

Congressional Index

CCH. [KF 4945]

This service covers each Congress and is a major finding tool for the current status of federal legislation. Bills are indexed by number, name, topic and sponsor. It does not contain the text of law. CCH also has a Legislative Reporting Service online which tracks bills. The print service is updated weekly during sessions.

United States Law Week

BNA. [KF 105]

This publishes all U.S. Supreme Court cases within a week of decision, provides a calendar of all Supreme Court activity (pending cases, etc.), reproduces selective excerpts of significant state and lower federal court opinion, provides general reviews of the activities of the courts, prints significant new laws, occasionally prints oral arguments before the Supreme Court, and provides extensive indexing. The service also covers the annual meetings of the major legal associations.

It is available online through BNA, Dialog, *LEXIS* and *WESTLAW*.

III. A SELECTION FOR THE PUBLIC ADMINISTRATOR

Accounting Articles

CCH. [HF 563]

A monthly updated loose-leaf providing indexing and summaries of accounting literature. See also *Accountant's Index* from the AICPA which appears quarterly covering 290 periodicals and *NEXIS* from Mead Data which provides full online accounting information services.

Administrative Practice Manual

BNA. [KF 5406]

This is a guide to the federal regulatory agencies, their procedures, staff, information disclosure requirements, etc. "In the midst of the surging sea of politics, policies, and personalities" (Preface), this service cites and explains relevant *Code of Federal Regulations*, *U.S. Code*, *Attorney General's Manual* and Administrative Procedures Act sections and suggests procedurial approaches, provides directory information, bibliographies, checklists, tables, fees.

Air & Water Pollution Control

BNA. [KF 3775]

Covers regulatory trends, control techniques, compliance practices and costs and thorough reference material on the topic. BNA publishes similar services on chemical regulations, hazardous materials, transport, noise, mine safety, etc., see *Environment Reporter BNA*.

All-States Tax Reports

BNA. [KF 1670]

Five volumes.

American Law of Zoning

Lawyers Co-Op. [KF 5698]

A four volume set updated with pocket parts.

Bender's Uniform Commercial Code Service.

Bender. [KF 885]

A comprehensive service in more than one hundred volumes, bound and loose-leaf. It provides text of the UCC as promulgated by the National Conference of Commissoners of Uniform State Law and cases and interpretation, along with a state correlation index and other indexes.

Civil Rights Actions

Bender. [KF 4749]

Covers civil action, including class actions, under civil rights legislation. Includes text of law and bibliographies.

Collective Bargaining Negotiations & Contracts

BNA. [KF 3408]

Comparative State Income Tax Guide with forms

Oceana. [KF 6752]

Condemnation Procedures & Techniques

Bender. [KF 5599]

Part three of the four volumes of *Real Estate Transactions* published by Bender. This part provides the background of eminent domain proceedings by federal, state and local agencies for various purposes especially now when condemnation applies to substantially improved property.

Condominium Law & Practice

Bender. [KF 581]

Another part of Bender's services covering real estate transactions.

Congressional Yellow Book

Monitor Publishing. [Reference]

Sketches of members of Congress, their staff, phone numbers, etc. Special paperback updating editions include state delegates, district maps and other congressional finding information.

Constitutions of the US: National & State

Oceana. [KF 4530]

Published for the Legislative Drafting Research Fund of Columbia University by Oceana.

Consumer Product Safety Guide

CCH. [KF 1606]

Cooperative Housing Law & Practice

Bender. [KF 623]

Another part of Bender's services covering real estate transactions.

Cost Accounting Standards Guide

CCH. [KF 846.5]

Directory of Labor Relations

Labor Relations Press. [KF 3421]

Employee and Union Member Guide to Labor Law

Boardman. [KF 3369]

A two volume manual for attorneys representing the labor movement from the National Lawyers Guild.

Employee Benefits Cases Service

BNA. [KF 3315]

Employee Benefits Compliance Coordinator

RIA. [KF 736]

Employment and Training Reporter

BNA. [KF 3775]

For those who plan, administer and coordinate job training programs, this service includes description of state and local policies and programs, reports and data on service delivery areas, state and local allocations, and labor force, enrollment and performance data. State laws and regulations are presented in synopses.

Employment Practices Guide

CCH. [KF 3464]

This service presents information on federal and state rules prohibiting discrimination in employment.

Employment Safety & Health Guide

CCH. [KF 3568.4]

Indexes and reports on standards, compliance rules, decisions and regulations under OSHA.

Environment Reporter

BNA. [KF 3775]

Twenty loose-leaf volumes, the leading information resource on national environment protection and pollution control; it includes coverage of state laws and regulation and directory to state agencies and personnel. Sections are available separately and are not listed here.

Equal Employment Opportunity Compliance Manual

P-H. [KF 3464]

Equal Opportunity in Housing

P-H. [KF 5740]

Ethics in Government Reporter

Washington Service Bureau. [KF 4568]

Covering political ethics, conflict of interest, campaign contributions, etc.

Exempt Organizations Reporter

CCH. [KF 6449]

This three volume service covers federal and state laws on incorporation, exemption, registration requirements and charitable contribution to the tax exempt private foundations, charities and trusts.

Fair Employment Practice Service

BNA. [KF 3314]

Fair Housing-Fair Lending

P-H. [KF 5740]

The legal requirements are indexed and set forth; cases may be looked up by type of discriminatory action.

Federal Contracts Report

BNA. [KF 846]

Reports on developments affecting federal contracts and grants and covers such issues as local procurement, allowable costs, appeals, etc. Tracks conference, committee hearings, deadlines, personnel changes, etc., and provides some background treatment and full text on major topics.

Federal Election Campaign Financing

CCH. [KF 4920]

Two volume set provides full text reporting on restrictions and limitations governing federal campaign financing.

Federal Employment Relations Manual

BNA. [KF 3409]

A one volume guidebook for the government manager documenting and explaining relevant law and administrative acts and bodies (Civil Service Reform Act of 1978, Federal Service Impasses Panel, Federal Mediation and Conciliation Service, etc.) and reports, discussion, guidelines, ect., based on actual arbitration decisions.

Federal Tax Articles

CCH. [KF 6335]

This service will also be found in many business libraries. It provides indexing and summaries of articles in law, business and academic journals on federal taxes.

Federal Taxation

CCH. [KF 6335]

The volumes in this looseleaf library are updated weekly and provide tax relevant statutory material, reprinting of each section of the tax code followed by regulations, digests of cases, annotation or explanation of key sections, key text of cases, finding lists, special tax releases containing new laws and bills, explanation of new laws, committee reports, studies, a short review of significant developments since last release, and instruction for use of the service.

Commerce Clearing House publishes over 250 topical law reporters covering all the major phases of tax and business law. As with the other major publishers, BNA and Prentice-Hall, they also provide online access to many reporters by special contract and, in the same manner, to research services.

Government Contracts Reporter

CCH. [KF 846]

A nine volume reporter covering the law and regulation surrounding government contract work. Historical and other permanent material is in the accompaning bound volumes.

Government Employee Relations Report

BNA. [KF 3580]

The reference volumes reprint documents on federal, state and local programs, on major issues, data such as detailed wage agreements and other contract provisions, and provides a contract clause finder and glossary. Current reports cover federal level union activitiers, rules and regulations, subject-related legislation. There is a case file, calendar of events, statistics and other reporting on the subject.

Guide to Municipal Official Statements

Law & Business. [KF 5315]

A guide for preparing municipal official financial statements required in the sale of municipal securities.

Guide to State Legislative Materials

Rothman. [KF 1]

The third edition was published in 1985 by Rothman for the American Association of Law Libraries.

Handicapped Americans Report

Business Publishers. [KF 480]

A biweekly updated loose-leaf covering the administrative, legislative and judicial developments affecting handicapped Americans. It includes handicapped rights and the regulations that apply to governmental and private entities.

Health Administration: Laws Regulations & Guidelines

National Health Publishing Corp. [KF 3821]

Health Care Labor Manual

Aspen Publishers. [KF 3580]

A labor relations guide for this area of employment. Non-legal material includes characteristics of the health care industry by particular employee categories, the history of organizing in the industry, information on labor organizations, summaries of law.

Hospital Cost Management

P-H. [RA 971]

This loose-leaf is a compilation of ideas and techniques currently in place for hospital cost containment.

Housing & Development Reporter

BNA. [KF 5726]

This provides directory information for the subject, including directories of housing and development organizations and official bodies. In the three Reference volumes there is very detailed treatment of HUD including historical background, programs, etc., and treatment of the public and private secondary mortgage programs and market, state housing finance agencies, etc. It covers financing and statutes, as well as reporting on law and regulations.

Human Resources Management

CCH. [KF 3455]

A five volume service covering employment relations, compensation, EEO and personnel practices. As with all the major labor relations services, consumer price index data, surveys of practices, data on trends and other reference material is included along with labor relation law and regulation.

Industrial Relations Guide

P-H. [KF 3366]

Labor Arbitration Awards

CCH. [KF 9085]

This is a widely held finder and text service for public and private arbitration awards.

Labor Arbitration Index

Labor Relations Publications. [KF 3421.5]

A comprehensive finder and text service for all public and private abbitration awards. It includes detailed one page biographies of labor arbitrators. Specialized searches of the database are available online from the publisher.

Labor Relations Reporter

BNA. [KF 3314]

BNA's comprehensive service covering labor-management relations (two volumes), fair employment practices (three volumes), arbitration (one volume), wages and hours (three volumes), rights (two volumes), etc. It covers state laws (two volumes), court and NLRB decisions (two volumes), and includes extensive indexing and reference information. This and other BNA services are available through *LEXIS, NEXIS, WESTLAW* and this service can be searched through Dialog file *LABORLAW.*

Law of Workman's Compensation

Bender. [KF 3613]

Local Government Law

Bender. [KF5300]

C.J. Antieau's compilation and commentary covers municipal corporations, independent local government entities and counties.

Municipal Ordinances

Callaghan. [KF 5313]

A practical guide, and a form book, to the drafting of ordinances.

National Public Employment Reporter

LRP. [KF 3580]

This is in two volumes. Labor Relations Press also publishes *FEDERAL PAY & BENEFITS REPORTER.*

Negotiated Employee Benefit Plans

Callaghan. [KF 3510]

NLRB Case Handling Manual

CCH. [KF 3372]

Occupational Safety & Health Reporter

BNA. [KF 3568]

The reference binders of this set include standards and regulations, NIOSH documents, state plans, directories, etc.

Pension Plan Guide

CCH. [KF 736]

Pension Reporter

BNA. [KF 3510]

Personnel Management

P-H. [KF 3365]

Policy & Practice Series

BNA. [KF 3812 or KF 3788]

Sets within the series include Personnel Management, Labor Relations, Wages and Hours, Compensation, and Fair Employment Practices. On major trends in compensation there will be explanation, illustration and survey of practices, suggestions for implimentation, publicity, cost analysis, etc. As with most such services, detailed CPI data is included.

Pollution Control Guide

CCH. [KF 3775]

Products Liability Reporter

CCH. [KF 1296]

Products Liability

Bender. [KF 1296]

An eight volume set.

Protection of Abused Victims; State Laws and Decisions

Oceana. [KF 9320]

This covers abuse of children, elderly and women by family members and caretaker institutions and, as well as statutes and decisions, provides extensive non-legal discussion of the issue.

Public Employee Bargaining

CCH. [KF 3409]

Three volumes and supplementary pamphlets and newsletter. This category of information is well serviced by several reporters. Since the Taft-Hartley and Landrum-Griffin Acts do not apply to public sector employees, it is a state issue and information is quite diverse. This is organized by subject (bargaining units, mediation/arbitration, etc.) with text of state law and regulations and decisional materials provided. It also provides bibliography, contract provisions, and sample material from organizing campaigns from both labor and management.

Public Employee Bargaining

CCH. [KF 3409]

In three volumes this provides full text reporting on law and regulations concerning public employee collective bargaining with state and local governments.

Public Personnel Administration-Policies & Practices for Personnel

P-H. [KF 3580]

This component of a discontinued larger service for personnel managers in the public sector covers techniques and requirements for organizing and administering such thing as position classification, personnel selection and training, promotions and wage and salary issues, benefits, discipline, etc.

Sales Taxes

P-H. [KF 1670]

Covers sales, use, receipts and related taxes for states, cities, counties and metropolitan areas.

School Law Register

Capitol. [KF 4115]

Covering education law, legislation and regulation.

Securities Regulation & Law Report

BNA. [KF 1439]

One of several services covering SEC rulemaking and related activity, this one includes analysis of trends in this area and state securities agency activities, decisions under state securities law and activities of the North American Securities Administrators Association.

Starting and Operating a Business in [State]

Oasis. [KFM 2634]

In addition to the relevant law and regulation, this provides directory information, bibliographies and other information.

State and Local Government Debt Financing

Callaghan. [KF 6724]

State and Local Taxes

P-H. [KF 6750]

State-specific editions of this service include the full text of statutes and regulations, court decisions and rulings. Prentice-Hall also has a state-specific set titled *STATE INCOME TAXES*.

State Tax Action Coordinator

RIA. [KF 6750]

A six volume service organized by region.

State Tax Guide

CCH. [KF 6750]

State Tax Reports

CCH. [KF 1670]

Separate sets for each state cover the entire field of the state and local taxation. CCH also publishes and *ALL-STATE SALES TAX REPORTS, STATE TAX CASES,* and other related state tax reporters.

Tax Exempt Organizations

P-H. [KF 6449]

> This and *Charitable Giving and Solicitation* P-H [KF 6388] cover the tax aspects for not-for-profit accountants, legal counsel and administrators.

Unemployment Insurance Reports

CCH. [KF 3673]

Workman's Compensation for Occupational Injuries & Death

Bender. [KF 3613]

Zoning & Land Use Controls

Bender. [KF 5698]

IV. MAJOR PUBLISHERS

Aspen . . . . (800)638-8437

Bender (Matthew Bender & Co.) . . . . (800)223-1940

BNA (Bureau of National Affairs . . . . (202)452-7889

Boardman (Clark Boardman Co.) . . . . . . (800)221-9428

Business Publication . . . . (800)323-4560

Callaghan & Co. . . . . (800)323-1336

Capitol . . . . (800)327-7203

CCH (Commerce Clearing House) . . . . . . (312)583-8500

Government Research Services . . . . (800)346-6898

Law & Business
(Harcourt Brace Jovanovich, Inc.) . . . . (800)223-0231

Lawyers Co-Op . . . . (800)527-0430

LRP (Labor Relations Press) . . . . (800)341-7874

Monitor Publishing Co. . . . . (212)627-4140

National Health Publishing . . . . (800)446-2221

Oasis Press . . . . (800)228-2275

Oceana . . . . (914)693-1733

P-H (Prentice-Hall Law & Business, Inc.) . . (800)223-0231

RIA (Research Insitute of America) . . . . . (800)431-2057

Rothman (Fred B. Rothman & Co.) . . . . . (800)457-1986

S&FA Reporting Services . . . . (703)739-0200

Part 7
ASSOCIATIONS AND INSTITUTES

There are a great many associations and agencies in the U.S. which serve the shared interests of professions and concerns within public administration. In this chapter we have identified some of the major organizations which maintain substantial libraries or accessible databases, publish major periodicals or in other ways are unique sources of information. Some are membership associations and are based on governmental units and others are associations serving a profession. Others are non-profit associations or institutes affiliated with universities, or not-for-profit organizations supported in various ways by research grants, fee-for-service activities, consulting and contract research. Most associations on the list below will provide a publication list on request. We list some of their recent publications only in order to illustrate the information activity of the association.

These titles do not necessarily appear in the indexes to the *Desk Book*.

To identify associations or institutes beyond this selected list, for instance to find the association serving your own field of work or supporting public administration research in your city or region, consult the following directories:

I. DIRECTORIES

Encyclopedia of Associations

24th ed. Detroit, MI: Gale Research Co., 1989.
Annual. Available online through Dialog.

This is the major directory and can be found in most libraries. There are name, key word, geographic and membership and staff size indexes. It is an excellent "switchboard" connecting persons needing information to persons in a position to provide it. The section "Legal, Governmental, Public Administrations and Military Organizations" describes over 1000 associations. International associations, regional associations and association research and funding programs are covered in separate volumes. Gale also publishes a directory of association periodicals in three volumes and an encyclopedia of governmental advisory organizations.

Online access to the *Encyclopedia of Associations* is obviously a most cost effective way for a small office to use such a massive directory. The directory is also available on CD-ROM at a cost about forty percent higher than the five volume print set. In print or on CD-ROM, your office is acquiring the entire database, information on more than 25,000 associations, whereas with the online service you download and pay for only the information you need.

Municipal Year Book 1989

Washington, DC: International City Management Association, 1989. Annual.

This authoritative source book of urban data and developments describes seventy-four professional, special assistance and education organizations serving local and state government. This source book is widely used; it is available in most libraries. Our selected list of associations is intended, in part, to supplement theirs. Together they do no more than indicate the variety of associations serving public administration.

National Trade and Professional Associations of the United States

24th ed. Washington, DC: Columbia Books, 1989. Annual.

Also valuable, especially for trade and professional associations in the Washington, DC area, this one volume directory has name, geographic, subject and budget size indexes. Its annotations on the associations it covers is as informative as the comparable notes in *Encyclopedia of Associations.* For a given annual edition, information is at least as current at that in the larger directory.

II. A SELECTION OF ORGANIZATIONS

ADVISORY COMMISSION ON INTERGOVERNMENTAL RELATIONS

Suite 2000, Vanguard Bldg.
1111 Twentieth St. NW
Washington, DC 20575
(202)653-5640

Created by Congress in 1959, this is not an membership association but a permanent and independent agency to study intergovernmental problems. It sponsors the quarterly *Intergovernmental Perspective*. Recent titles from its extensive publication activity are:

Hearings on Constitutional Reform of Federalism,
1989.

Metropolitan Organization, 1988.

The Tax Reform Act of 1986, 1988.

Public Assistance in the Federal System, 1988.

Metropolitan Organization; the St. Louis Case, 1988.

Significant Features of Fiscal Federalism, annual.

State Fiscal Capacity and Effort, annual.

The Organization of Local Public Economies, 1987.

AMERICAN ACCOUNTING ASSOCIATION

5717 Bessie Drive
Sarasota, FL 33583
(813)921-7747

Publishes the quarterly *Accounting Review* which focuses on accounting education and publishes accounting research articles, usually quantitative analysis of interest to the research-oriented academic audience. *Auditing* is published twice a year by the auditing section of the association; it focuses on auditing procedures and practices. The association plays a major role in the development of accounting education; its Government and Nonprofit Section is important in developing standards and information sources for public and non-profit accounting. See:

> *Governmental Accounting, Auditing, and Financial Reporting*, 1988.

> *An Annotated Bibliography of Articles; Government Accounting, Auditing, and Municipal Finance, 1971-1985*, 1986.

> *An Inventory of Data Sources for Governmental and Other Nonprofit Organizations*, 1985.

AMERICAN ASSOCIATION OF SMALL CITIES

Route 2, P.O. Box 128
DeLeon, TX 76444
(817)893-5818

Members are cities, towns and townships, villages, hamlets and boroughs having a population of less than 50,000. Maintains service centers in ten states. Publications include *Newsletter*, monthly, and *Special Reports*, semiannual; also publishes monographs.

ASSOCIATED PUBLIC-SAFETY COMMUNICATIONS OFFICERS

P.O. Box 669
New Smyrna Beach, FL 32070
(904)427-3461

Members are employees of public safety agencies involved with mobile land radio communications within and between agencies and governmental units. Sponsors an annual public safety equipment show. Periodicals are *APCO Reports*, monthly, *Journal of Public Safety Communications*, monthly, *APCO Bulletin*, 11/year. They also

publish operating procedure manuals, police telecommunications systems texts, signal cards and other material.

They publish the *Public Safety Communications Standard Operating Procedure Manual*, 21st ed., 1986.

AMERICAN BAR ASSOCIATION

750 N. Lake Shore Drive
Chicago, IL 60611
(312)988-5000

There are bar associations in every state and city and
they often maintain or are affiliated with accessible law
libraries. They often maintain legal referral services including referral to legal research and consultation services. The ABA has a Section of Urban, State and Local
Government whose publications are of interest to public
administrators. The national association plays a very
important role in legal education.

AMERICAN INSTITUTE OF CERTIFIED PUBLIC ACCOUNTANTS

1211 Avenue of the Americas
New York, NY 10036
(212)575-6200

This is a major center of accounting information. The
institute publishes periodicals: *Tax Advisor, CPA Letter,
Journal of Accountancy* and *Accountant's Index* which is
a major indexing of accounting literature. The AICPA
library is extensive, including all material indexed in
Accountant's Index, the material is available for loan to
members. Recent publications include:

Audits of Certain Nonprofit Organizations, 1988.

Audits of Airlines, 1988.

Audits of Voluntary Health and Welfare
Organizations, 1988.

AMERICAN PLANNING ASSOCIATION

1776 Massachusetts Avenue, NW
Washington, DC 20036
(202)872-0611

This association includes both public and private planning officials and personnel. It specializes in providing training services for the profession and acting as an information clearinghouse and referral service. It maintains an extensive library including a collection of zoning ordinances and decisions. The scope of the association extends beyond land use and zoning. Periodicals are: *Journal of the American Planning Association,* a quarterly; *Land Use and Zoning Digest* and *Planning Magazine,* a monthly.

AMERICAN PUBLIC WORKS ASSOCIATION

1313 E. 60th St.
Chicago, IL 60637
(312)667-2200

Members are chief administrators of public works, city engineers, superintendents and department heads, federal and state administrators and engineers, consultants and educators. Associate members are equipment manufacturers representatives, utility company officials and contractors. Operates a computerized local government information network; maintains a library of books and periodicals on public works. The association regularly publishes the *APWA Reporter,* a monthly, and an annual *Policy Statements.* It also publishes a directory, books, manuals, and special reports.

AMERICAN SOCIETY FOR PUBLIC ADMINISTRATION

1120 G St., N.W.
Washington, DC 20005
(202)393-7878

Members are professional governmental administrators, public officials, educators and others in related fields interested in public management as a career or profession. The major periodicals of this association are *Public Administration Times*, a biweekly, and *Public Administration Review*, a bimonthly.

The Association's Section on Personnel Administration and Labor Relations has recently produced studies on salary structure and merit pay, on gender bias in public employment, on civil service reform and similar topics. The association sponsors numerous individually authored studies dealing with program evaluation, intergovernmental relations, standards and ethics, the state of the profession, etc. Recent titles include:

Section on Science and Technology in Government, Statement on Science and Technology, 1989.

Accounting and Accountability in Public Administration, 1988.

Looking Back, Moving Forward; A Half-Century Celebration of Public Administration and ASPA, 1988.

AMERICAN WATER WORKS ASSOCIATION

6666 W. Quincy Ave.
Denver, CO 80235
(303)794-7711

Members are water utility officials, managers, engineers, chemists and others; water departments, boards of health, manufacturers and consultants. The association maintains a technical library and information center on the water utilities industry and the online database

WATERNET, available from Dialog, which indexes over 16,000 technical reports and studies from the association, regulatory agencies and other sources as well as manuals, standards, test method literature and the contents of *Journal of the American Water Works Association*. Other periodicals are: *Community Relations Newsletter, Mainstream, Washington Report, WaterWorld News*.

ASSOCIATION OF GOVERNMENT ACCOUNTANTS

727 S. 23rd St., Suite 100
Arlington, VA 22202
(703)684-6931

Members are accountants, auditors, comptrollers and budget officers employed by federal, state and local governments in management and administrative positions. Periodicals include *Government Financial Management Topics*, a monthly, and *Government Accountants Journal*, a quarterly.

COUNCIL OF STATE GOVERNMENTS

P.O. Box 11910, Iron Works Pike
Lexington, KY 40578
(606)252-2291

This major organization maintains a library collection of state government department and agency reports, large-scale survey responses on financial reporting issues and other documents from which material in *Book of the States* is selected. Periodicals are: *Backgrounders*, monthly; *State Government News*, monthly; *State Government Research Checklist*, bimonthly; *State Government*, quarterly. Also published are major reference tools: *The Book of the States*, biennial; *State Administrative Officials Classified by Functions*, biennial; *State Elective Officials and the Legislatures*, biennial; *State Legislative Leadership Committees and Staff*, biennial; *Legislative Research Checklist*. They also publish special reports on programs of state governments and their agencies.

GOVERNMENT FINANCE OFFICERS ASSOCIATION

180 N. Michigan Ave., Suite 800
Chicago, IL 60601
(312)977-9700

and also

1750 K Street, NW, Suite 200
Washington, DC 20006
(202)429-2750

This is a major center of information on governmental finance. Members are finance officers of governments and nonprofit institutions, public accounting firms, financial institutions and others. Periodical publications include a newsletter, *GAAFR Review* and *Public Investor*, both monthly, *Governmental Finance*, a quarterly, *Government Finance Review*, a quarterly. *Resources in Review*, a valuable newsletter survey of current literature, now appears as part of *Government Finance Review* where it provides announcements, reviews and abstracts of new literature appearing on the subject. The association also publishes a membership directory, special bulletins, textbooks and reports focusing on various areas of public financial management. They maintain a library collection of the annual reports of the more than 800 governmental units that have applied for the GFOA "Certificate of Conformance." The GFOA is the publisher of the important *Governmental Accounting, Auditing, and Financial Reporting*, 1988. Other recent publications include:

> *Credit Pooling to Finance Infrastructure: an Examination of State Bond Banks, State Revolving Funds and Substate Credit Pools*, 1988.

> *The Federal Taxation of Public Employee Retirement Systems; a Handbook for Public Officials*, 1988.

> *Government Fixed Asset Inventory Systems*, 1987.

INTERNATIONAL ASSOCIATION OF ASSESSING OFFICERS

1313 E. 60th Street
Chicago, IL 60637
(312)947-2069

An association of state and local officials concerned with property valuation. The association maintains a library and makes available research and consulting services. Publications include: *Assessment and Valuation Legal Reporter*, a monthly, *Assessment Digest*, a bimonthly, *Assessor's Data Exchange*, a quarterly, *Property Tax Journal*, quarterly; and a bibliographic series which includes:

Standard on Facilities, Computers, Equipment, and Supplies, 1989.

Introduction to the Assessment Profession, 1987.

The Valuation of Commercial Services Property: a Classified Annotated Bibliography, 1985 with supplements.

Computer-assisted Appraisal and Assessment Systems: an Annotated Bibliography, 1983 with supplements.

INTERNATIONAL ASSOCIATION OF MUNICIPAL CLERKS

160 North Altadena Drive
Pasadena, CA 91107
(818)795-6153

This professional asociation of 84,000 clerks, city secretaries and counsels sponsors educational programs at universities around the country and provides research, salary survey and other information services to the profession. The information is published in newsletters and technical bulletins for members. There is an annual directory of members which also lists affilitated state organizations.

INTERNATIONAL CITY MANAGEMENT ASSOCIATION

1120 G Street, N.W.
Washington, DC 20005
(202)626-4600

The association is a major information provider. Their publications are the *ICMA Newsletter*, biweekly, *Management Information Service Report*, monthly; *Public Management*, monthly; *Guide to Management Improvement Projects in Local Government*, quarterly, *Baseline Data Reports* and *Municipal Year Book*. They also publish special reports on municipal problems and training manuals for municipal departments. Recent publications include:

Software Reference Guide, 1988.

Managing Fire Services, 1988.

The Practice of Local Government Planning, 1988.

Developing Work Procedures, 1987.

Hazardous Materials, Hazardous Waste: Local Management Options, 1987.

FYI.. Resources on Local Government, 1983-1986, 1987.

Compensation Eighty-Seven: A Report on Local Government Executive Salaries & Fringe Benefits, 1987.

Code Administration & Enforcement: Problems & Promises, 1987.

INTERNATIONAL MUNICIPAL SIGNAL ASSOCIATION

P.O. Box 539
Newark, NY 14513
(315)331-2182

Members are professional organizations of government officials responsible for municipal signaling, alarms, communication, lighting, signs, etc. Publications include a bimonthly journal and *Traffic Signal Manual of Installation and Maintenance Procedures, Fire Alarm Manual, and Wire and Cable Specifications* and similar publications.

NATIONAL ASSOCIATION FOR STATE INFORMATION SYSTEMS

P.O. Box 11910, Iron Works Pike
Lexington, KY 40578
(606)254-7017

This is not a membership organization. Beginning in 1970 this association, a group within the Council of State Governments, published an annual *Information Systems Technology in State Governments*, which includes extensive tables of data from questionnaires to the states on the adoption of information technology. The most recent edition seen was 1986.

NATIONAL ASSOCIATION OF ATTORNEYS GENERAL

444 N. Capitol St.
Washington, DC 20001
(202)628-0435

Association publications include: *Antitrust Report*; *Consumer Protection Report, Criminal Justice Report*; *Environment Protection Report*; all are monthly. Also they publish *Medicaid Fraud Report* ten time a year and *Directory of Attorneys General of the States and Other Jurisdictions*, biennial.

NATIONAL ASSOCIATION OF COUNTIES

440 First St., N.W.
Washington, DC 20001
(202)393-6226

Members are elected and appointed county governing officials and other county officials and their deputies in management or policy making. The association's substantial staff provides staff support for affiliated state county associations and other professional organizations which, in turn, generate a large number of county affairs-focused publications. The association publishes through a non-profit corporation and a foundation of the same name.

NATIONAL CENTER FOR STATE COURTS

300 Newport Ave.
Williamsburg, VA 23185
(804)253-2000

This information center for the states' court systems maintains a 10,000 volume special library. Its periodical publications include: *Master Calendar*, monthly; *Report* (newsletter), monthly; *State Court Journal*, quarterly; *Judicial Salary Survey*, semiannual; *Annual Report*. It also publishes reports, briefing papers, pamphlets and books.
Publications include:

Child Support Guidelines Summery, 1989.

Status of State Financing of Courts: 1988, 1989.

NATIONAL CIVIC LEAGUE

1601 Grant St., Suite 250
Denver, CO 80203
(303)832-5615

Formerly National Municipal League. Members are civic leaders, educators, public officials, civic organizations, libraries and businesses. The association maintains a large library with a strong state constitution collection. A computerized service, *CIVITEX* (Civic Information and Techniques Exchange), can be searched to answer phone queries. Periodicals are *National Civic Review*, 6/year, and *Civic Action*, a newsletter. Recent publications sponsored by the league include a model county charter and the following:

Cities of Opportunity, 1988.

Local Government Internal Controls: A Guide for Public Officials, 1983.

Refuse Collection in New York State, 1980.

NATIONAL CONFERENCE OF STATE LEGISLATURES

1050 17th St., Suite 2100
Denver, CO 80265
(303)623-7800

This is a national organization of state legislators and legislative staff. Periodicals include *State Legislatures*, which appears ten times a year and *Conference Report*, a quarterly. The body also publishes a *State Legislative Report* and books, reports, guides, handbooks and films.

NATIONAL CONFERENCE OF COMMISSIONERS ON UNIFORM STATE LAWS

645 N. Michigan Ave.
Chicago, IL 60611
(312)321-9710

Members are judges, law school deans and professors and practicing attorneys appointed by state governors. Publications include *Handbook and Proceedings*, annual, and reference books and pamphlets on uniform laws and model acts adopted by the Conference.

NATIONAL GOVERNORS ASSOCIATION

444 N. Capitol Street, Suite 250
Washington, DC 20001
(202)624-5300

This association serves as a clearinghouse for information and ideas on the resolution of state and national issues. Publications include *Governors Bulletin*, a weekly, *Policy Positions*, semiannual, *Governors of American States, Commonwealths, Territories*, annual, and *Capital*

Ideas, bi-monthly, and a *Directory of Staff Assistants to the Governors*, biannual. The association also publishes monographs.

Recent publications include:

Restructuring the Schools; the Role of Paraprofessionals, 1989.

Restructuring in Progress; Lessons from Pioneering Districts, 1989.

State-financed, Workplace-based Retraining Programs, 1989.

Controlling Toxic Pollution; a Profile of State Activities, 1988.

New Business, Entrepreneurship, and Rural Development, 1988.

NATIONAL LEAGUE OF CITIES

1301 Pennsylvania Ave., N.W.
Washington, DC 20004
(202)626-3000

This major information provider is a federation of 49 state leagues and 1,126 cities and towns. It maintains a 20,000 volume library. Publications include *Nation's Cities Weekly*, *Urban Affairs Abstracts*, also weekly with semiannual and annual cumulations, *Directory of Local Officials*, a semiannual, *National Municipal Policy*, an annual, and *Resource Recovery Magazine*, a bi-monthly. Under the name *LOCAL EXCHANGE*, the National League of Cities provides on-line access to *Urban Affairs Abstracts* and through bulletin board and E-mail services gives access to their library and research services for members and subscribers. For information on the latter: (202) 627-3180.

PUBLIC SECURITIES ASSOCIATION

40 Broad St, 12th Floor
New York, NY 10004-2373
(212)809-7000

Members are banks and dealers that underwrite, trade and sell U.S. government and federal agency securities and state and local government securities. Computerized services include a database on new issues of municipal securities. Publications include: *Government Securities Newsletter*, monthly; *Mortgage-Backed Securities Newsletter*, monthly; *Municipal Securities Newsletter*, monthly; *Municipal Market Developments*, quarterly; *Statistical Yearbook of Municipal Finance*, annual. They also publish a Washington newsletter and such publication as *An Investor's Guide to Tax Exempt Securities*, *An Investor's Guide to Tax Exempt Unit Investment Trusts*, *Fundamentals of Municipal Bonds* and *Tax Exempt Versus Taxable Securities: A Comparison of Yields*.

PUBLIC TECHNOLOGY, INC.

1301 Pennsylvania Ave., N.W.
Washington, DC 20004
(202)626-2400

Members are local governments supporting research and development activities for cities and counties. It is affiliated with the National League of Cities. Publishes technical manuals and an annual catalog of programs, services and publications. Example of their recent publication are:

Flexible Design Standards for Highway Improvements, 1988.

Local Government & AIDS; a Special Report with Case Studies, 1988.

RFPs for Computer-Aided Dispatching, 1988.

SOUTHERN BUILDING CODE CONGRESS, INTERNATIONAL

900 Montclair Rd.
Birmingham, AL 35213
(205)591-1853

Members are state, county, municipal, or other government subdivisions; associate members are trade associations, architects, engineers, contractors and related groups. Publication include: *Southern Building Magazine*, bimonthly; *Membership Directory*, annual; *Standard Building Code*, triennial; *Standard Fire Prevention Code*, triennial; *Standard Gas Code*, triennial; *Standard Mechanical Code*, triennial; *Standard Plumbing Code*, triennial.

SPECIAL LIBRARIES ASSOCIATION

1700 18th Street, N.W.
Washington, DC 20009
(202)234-4700

Several divisions of this association publish valuable reference tools, such as the Employee Benefits Division's *Insurance Periodicals Index* covering thirty-seven journals in insurance and benefits. They publish *Special Libraries*, a quarterly and *SpeciaList*, a monthly containing news about members.

UNITED STATES CONFERENCE OF MAYORS

1620 Eye St., N.W.
Washington, DC 20006
(202)293-7330

Members are mayors of cities of more than 30,000 population, represented by their mayors. Publications are: *The Mayor*, semimonthly; *Network*, monthly; *Partnership: Chronicling Public/Private Collaborations*, monthly; *The Mayors of America's Principal Cities*, semiannual; *City Problems*, annual; and *The Federal Budget and the Cities*.

URBAN INSTITUTE

2100 M Street, N.W.
Washington, D.C. 20037
(202)833-7200

Like the Advisory Commission on Intergovernmental Relations included here, the Urban Institute is not a membership organization. It is the recipient of substantial grants from private foundations and public sources to perform research on domestic policy issues, including finance, health, housing, social welfare and economic development. It also performs evaluation studies of public programs. Most grants include provision for preparing publications which are often co-sponsored by public administration associations. Its publication list is extensive. Recent publications include:

Program Analysis for State & Local Governments, 1989.

Guide to the Federal Budget: Fiscal 1989, 1988.

Challenge to Leadership: Social & Economic Issues for the Next Decade, 1988.

Directory of Incentives for Business Investment & Development, 1986.

Appendix A
A BASIC LIBRARY

The following books are those we believe will be used repeatedly in even the smallest information center serving public administration practitioners.

Almanac of American Politics

Washington, DC: National Journal, 1989. Biennial.

The main body of this work is an examination of each state's political status, a short history and a narrative concerning the current governor, congressional representatives and presidential politics. Statistics are provided on the state population, the state share of federal tax burden and expenditure and on recent presidential elections. Each member of Congress is discussed and ratings by several national political action organizations and associations are given. Information on campaign funding is also included. Each congressional representative's district is examined in a narrative preceding the numeric data. Senate and House committees and subcommittees and their members are listed near the end of this work. There are several comparative charts ranking states and a chart of the top ten fund raisers by chamber and of the financial activity of the two major party organizations. A comprehensive combined personal name and subject index completes the work.

Book of the States

Lexington, KY: The Council of State Governments, 1988-89. Biennial.

An important reference tool containing state data and text chapters discussing unfolding state developments. There are ten chapters on the states: Constitutions; Executive Branch; Legislative Branch; Judicial Branch; Elections; Finances; Management and Administration; Selected Activities, Issues and Services; Intergovernmental Affairs; and statistics and information. There is an effort to balance the data tables and statistics with meaningful subject articles. There is no other reference tool which provides in one place the same topic coverage and depth as this publication. Original sources of information is indicated on the tables.

County and City Data Book

1988. Washington, DC: Department of Commerce, Bureau of the Census, 1988.

These are statistics compiled by federal agencies and departments arranged by counties, cities and towns with 25,000 or more inhabitants and places with 2,500 or more inhabitants, presented alphabetically by state within the statistical subject area. It is published as a supplement to the *Statistical Abstract*.

Current Municipal Problems

A quarterly, with annual cumulation, from Callaghan & Co.

The selection of periodicals valuable to a specific public administration information center is based on interests unique to each center; therefore, we do not try to select them here. This compilation, however, captures such interesting and valuable material from such far-flung and thinly distributed publications that we wanted to include it here. In any context where any one of the practitioner-oriented municipal magazines is read, this publication will be a valuable addition. It reprints articles selected from these magazines nationwide, about 100 per year. Many of the articles would, otherwise, remain inaccessible.

Economic Report of the President, Together with the Annual Report of the Council of Economic Advisers

Washington, DC: U.S. Government Printing Office, 1988. Annual.

This economic report, submitted each February, is a valuable compilation of information. It includes discussion and data on the performance and prospects of the economy. Statistical tables relating to employment, personal income, production, foreign trade and other issues are presented. These are usually time-series presentations; they are from a variety of governmental and non-governmental agencies and organizations.

Facts and Figures on Government Finance, 1988-89

24th ed. Washington, DC: Tax Foundation; Baltimore, MD: Johns Hopkins University Press, 1988. Biennial.

This is a very handy information service which includes 283 tables of financial data documenting the taxing and spending activities at federal, state and local levels. Where appropriate, data includes time series presentations so that trends can be identified and studied. Sources of data are explained in an introduction to the tables and source of further information is included with each table. A glossary of terms with brief annotations is included.

Municipal Year Book 1989

Washington, DC: International City Management Association, 1989. Annual.

An authoritative and indispensable annual source book on municipal data and development. In most years, the fifth chapter includes the directories of officials in local government. Numerous directories are included: state municipal leagues; state agencies for community affairs; state municipal management associations; state associations of counties; directors of councils of government; selected county officials; and elected municipal officials. An annotated directory of professional, special assistance and educational organizations serving local and state governments is also included. Most state municipal leagues are identified in this publication. The bibliography of reference tools, handbooks and other literature is excellent and frequently updated.

National Trade and Professional Associations of the United States

24th ed. Washington, DC: Columbia Books Inc., 1989. Annual.

This is an inexpensive directory of over six thousand trade associations, labor unions and professional and other non-profit voluntary associations. The citations are as adequate as those in *Encyclopedia of Associations*, with twenty-two thousand national associations, and there are subject, geographic, budget and executive indexes. For bodies in the Washington, DC area, this directory is nearly comprehensive.

Public Administration Desk Book

Newton Center, MA: Government Research Publications, 1990.

A guide to the reference tools, including online services and machine-readable files, useful to the public administration researcher or practitioner. The text and a special appendix identify more specialized finding tools, should they be needed. A detailed subject index provides titles and additional information so that the index alone stands as a valuable key to finding information.

State Legislative Leadership, Committees & Staff 1987-88

Lexington, KY: The Council on State Governments, 1987. Biennial.

Identifies legislative officers (such as Speaker of the House, majority and minority leaders, etc.) and staff services (such as House Clerk) for each state. Also identifies all standing and joint legislative committees and chairpersons. Legislative agencies are also listed. Addresses and telephone numbers are included. Appendices include selected officers and their addresses for the Senate and the House. There are several appendices identifying selected committees arranged by Committee subject area such as "Agriculture" and then by state, listing the committee Chairperson. Other appendices identify Legislative Reference Libraries and Legislative Service Agencies, both arranged by state.

Statistical Abstract of the United States 1989

109th edition. Washington, DC: U.S. Bureau of the Census, 1989. Annual.

The *Statistical Abstract of the United States* has been published annually since 1878 and is the standard summary of statistics on the social, political and economic organization of the United States. Its hundreds of tables are distributed through more than thirty sections divided by subject areas such as vital statistics, elections and manufacturers. A detailed subject index facilitates access to the data.

It is truly an index to and abstract of the wealth of national statistics providing not just data but detailed reference to fuller or more comprehensive sources of data.

Survey of Current Business

Monthly from the U.S. Bureau of Economic Analysis.

This monthly publication is the most important single source for estimates and analyses of U.S. economic activity and current U.S. business statistics. Each issue includes a narrative on the "Business Situation" which contains statistical data. Statistical tables are also provided for selected national income and product accounts and composite indexes of leading, coincident and lagging indicators. Each issue then presents as many as five topical articles with statistical tables. Usually during the course of the calendar year several articles will appear with statistical tables concerning governmental finances and fiscal conditions.

United States Government Manual 1988/89

Washington, DC: Office of the Federal Register National Archives and Records Administration, 1988. Annual.

This official handbook of the federal government provides comprehensive information on the agencies of the legislative, judicial and executive branches, including citations for enabling legislation or authority, primary functions, responsibilities and identifying key officials. Organizational charts are also included. The manual includes information on the quasi-official agencies, international organizations in which the United States participates, boards, committees and commissions.

Useful appendices include commonly used abbreviations and acronyms, as well as executive agencies which have been terminated, transferred or changed names since 1933. Separate indexes are included for personal names and agency or subject.

World Almanac and Book of Facts, 1989

New York: Pharos Books, 1989.

Published annually since 1868, the *World Almanac* is a general reference tool which provides brief information, usually by lists and charts, on thousands of topics. Often used as a starting place in seeking information, there is usually an indication of the original source of the facts presented.

Appendix B
OTHER GUIDES TO PUBLIC ADMINISTRATION INFORMATION

This Appendix describes published guides to information sources for public administration. The works here perform a service similar to that of our *Desk Book*, or would appear to do so. Although many are out of date they may assist the reader in identifying information resources in the history of public administration, comparative public administration and in methods of research. In some instances they cover a particular field in much greater detail than this *Desk Book*.

American Public Administration

Gerald E. Caiden, et al. *New York: Garland Publishing, Inc., 1983.*

This bibliographic guide identifies 1,200 sources by subject or specialty. There is an introductory essay on the scope of public administration and a second chapter on abstracts, indexes and continuing bibliographies. There is a chapter on periodicals with annotations designed for publishing scholars. Another chapter includes unannotated lists of nearly a thousand public administration studies arranged into six general sections including: classic texts in American public administration, 1890-1960; core texts; general anthologies; bibliographies, case studies, and workbooks; frequently cited contemporary texts; and specialized bibliographies.

Business Information Sources

Rev ed. Lorna M. Daniells. Berkeley, CA: University of California Press, 1985.

This is the best available guide to business reference sources. Lorna M. Daniells is bibliographer for the library of the Harvard Business School. Citations and descriptive annotations cover the major professional business information services, as of the date of this guide, along with major texts, handbooks and periodicals. There is a chapter concerning management of public and nonprofit organizations. There is a combined author, title and subject index. This tool also appears in machine-readable form in the *Microsoft Bookshelf*, a CD-ROM product containing a dictionary, thesaurus, world almanac, ZIP code directory, manual of style and others volumes.

Comparative Public Administration: An Annotated Bibliography

Mark W. Huddleston. New York, NY: Garland Publishing, Inc., 1984.

This is an annotated bibliography of over six hundred books and journal articles, from seventy journals, published between 1962 and 1981 on comparative public administration. The annotations are divided into nine chapters by topic, such as Bureaucracy and Politics, Public Budgeting, Local and Field Administration and Personnel Administration.

Encyclopedia of Business Information Sources

6th ed. and supplement. Edited by James Woy. Detroit, MI: Gale Research Company, 1986.

Although primarily intended for the business professional, this bibliography will be useful to those in the public sector as well. This work uncritically cites informational sources in over a thousand topic areas. Sources include abstracting services and indexes; bibliographies; encyclopedias and dictionaries; handbooks and manuals; online data bases, statistical sources; and other informational sources. Topical areas of potential interest to the public administrator include: auditing; city planning; government bonds; municipal government; property taxes; urban development; valuation; and others. There are no annotations and it is useful mainly as a check on additional sources of information beyond Daniells' *Business Information Sources.*

Encyclopedia of Public Affairs Information Sources

1st ed. Edited by Paul Wasserman. Detroit, MI: Gale Research Company, 1988.

This guide provides eight thousand unannotated citations to sources of information on public affairs. It is arranged into nearly three hundred subject areas; there are no indexes. It appears to have been assembled electronically from the numerous other Gale Research Company reference tools and can serve as a check on additional sources of information beyond those of a more selective, annotated guide.

Federal Information Sources in Health and Medicine

Mary Glen Chitty. New York: Greenwood Press, 1988.

This annotated bibliography directs attention to the many medical and health databases and statistical publications of the federal government. It annotates about 1200 government publications and for this subject is a unique and valuable guide to sources of information.

FYI... Resources on Local Government, 1983-85

Washington, D.C.: International City Management Association, 1986.

A bibliography of monographs, books, periodicals, and reports published between 1983 and 1985 relating to local government. In seventeen subject chapters, it gathers citations and to books, reports, monographs, bibliographies reference sources and periodicals. It is one of the few guides to the literature which has a practitioner orientation, including among its subjects, fire protection, housing, utilities, recreation, transportation.

Guide to Library Research in Public Administration

Antony E. Simpson. New York: Center for Productive Public Management, John Jay College of Criminal Justice, 1976.

Although essentially an annotated bibliography, and quite out of date, Simpson's guide provides the user with effective instruction in how to use a university library and its collection for academic public administration research.

The guide discusses and annotates informational sources such as special studies, essays, pamphlets, technical reports, dissertations, yearbooks, annual reviews and unpublished information. The text tends to be critical and analytical as differences between resources are pointed out and the author frequently makes recommendations as to the most useful sources. Simpson provides the user with a lesson on how to use a library card catalog and discusses the importance of library archives for research. The guide has a combined author, title and subject index.

Guide to Public Administration

D.A. Cutchin. Itasca, IL: F.E. Peacock Publishers, Inc., 1981.

A guide which is part dictionary, part handbook and part guide to the literature. One section is an annotated bibliography of research sources and journals and abstracts. Another is an alphabetical arrangement of definitions and explanations of concepts, theories, and facts. Another includes brief annotations of research sources including: bibliographies; directories; general reference works; handbooks on fiscal policy; laws and regulations and taxes; indexes; and statistics. Another section is an annotated bibliography of journals and abstracts. The last section includes organizational charts of the Executive Branch Departments reprinted from the *U.S. Government Organization Manual*. There is a subject index.

Guide to the Foundations of Public Administration

Daniel W. Martin. New York: Marcel Dekker, Inc., 1989.

This new addition to the Public Administration and Public Policy series of the publisher is a critical, annotated bibliographic guide to the major literature in American public administration. By this we mean that it presents the classic theoretical literature. Under subject chapters, the literature is described as it developed chronologically.

Thus, seminal and influential works (including articles, special studies, reports and textbooks) are presented in synopses to make a readable, consecutive description of thinking in this field.

Handbook of Information Sources and Research Strategies in Public Administration

Mary G. Rock. San Diego, CA: Institute of Public and Urban Affairs, San Diego State University, 1979.

Unlike Simpson's guide described here, this handbooks is intended for the student and practitioner, not the graduate student and academic scholar. It annotates and describes public administration information print sources in six major areas: basic books as texts and readers; major reference sources including yearbooks, statistical compilations, encyclopedias, handbooks and dictionaries; bibliographies; periodicals and indexing and abstracting tools; thirty-eight major organizations in public administration including their concepts, function, role and specific publications; and federal, state and local documents. The role and importance of each type of source is discussed.

How to Find the Law

7th ed. Morris L. Cohen St. Paul, MN: West Publishing Co., 1976.

Although primarily designed as a teaching tool, this resource may be used as a reference source on how to conduct legal research for someone trying to access the law. It is more than a bibliography which identifies the necessary legal reference tools. It takes the reader through the use of each of the major resources and carefully describes how some of these tools can be used cooperatively with one another.

Information Sources of Political Science

4th ed. Frederick L. Holler. Santa Barbara, CA: ABC-Clio, Inc., 1986.

An annotated bibliography of information sources relevant to the study of political science in a university library. Part II of this work is divided into seven chapters which provide annotated entries of information in: general reference sources; social sciences, including economics, education, political science, and psychology; American government, politics, and public law; international relations and organizations; comparative and area studies of politics and government; political theory; and public administration. Sources cited and annotated include bibliographies, dictionaries, casebooks, encyclopedias, handbooks, yearbooks, and online databases.

Program Evaluation: An Annotated Bibliography

Patrick S. Dynes and Mary K. Marvel. New York, NY: Garland Publishing, Inc., 1987.

An annotated bibliography of nearly four hundred fifty articles and studies, dissertations, and books published between 1970 and 1985 concerning program evaluation in public administration. The annotations are divided into four chapters: historical trends in evaluation research, methodological issues, organization and management issues, and sources discussing the degree to which the results of evaluation are utilized.

Public Administration in American Society: A Guide to Information Sources

John E. Rouse, Jr. Detroit, MI: Gale Research Company, 1980.

This guide covers a very wide assortment of sources including books, book chapters, reports and articles in periodicals. Article citations dominate and the work has become out of date. Effective use of the online periodical indexes make consulting works which are largely lists of articles unnecessary.

Public Administration: A Guide to the Literature

Howard E. McCurdy. New York: Marcel Dekker, Inc., 1986.

What this volume does is identify and annotate the one hundred and eighty-one public administration textbooks and special studies which are most frequently cited in forty reading lists gathered by the author. The works identified were published from the late 1960's into the 1980's. Along with the bibliographic citation is a brief assessment of the work's contribution to the field. There is an additional list, without annotations, of books cited at least two or three times. These are arranged into thirty three subject categories.

Public Finance: An Information Sourcebook

Marion B. Marshall. Phoenix, AZ: Oryx Press, 1987.

A well organized annotated bibliography of journal articles, books, and reports on public finance, the study of economics in the public sector. There are over a thousand citations with annotations varying in length from one to several sentences. Citations are arranged within subject headings for: Public Finance; Financial Management; Federal Government Finances; Federal Tax Policy; Federal Government Revenues; Information Sources on the Federal Government, which is organized into types of information sources such as documents and databases; Intergovernmental Fiscal Relations; State-Local Finances; State-Local Revenues; State-Local Financial Management; and Government Expenditures. There are separate author, title, and subject indexes.

Recent Publications on Governmental Problems

Monthly from the Merriam Center Library, Chicago, IL.

Many libraries hold this useful monthly listing. It includes published books, monographs, government documents and guides and other publications of public and private agencies. Its coverage also includes selected articles from approximately three hundred periodicals. Each issue is organized into ten general headings, with citations arranged under subheadings.

Searching the Law

Edward J. Bander, Frank Bae and Francis A. Doyle. Dobbs Ferry, NY: Transnational Publishers, 1987.

This valuable book is organized by subject and includes under each subject the major professional legal services, the looseleafs, online services, periodicals and introductory and overview books for that topic.

State Government Research Checklist

Bimonthly from the Council of State Governments.

Similar to *Recent Publications on Governmental Problems*, this is a list, arranged by subject headings, of documents received by The Council of State Governments. Most of the documents are generated by the various departments and agencies of the fifty states; however, useful resources from national and non-profit associations and organizations are also included. The citations are unannotated.

State Legislatures

Robert U. Goehlert and Frederick W. Musto. Santa Barbara, CA: ABC-Clio Information Services, 1985.

An unannotated bibliography of over 2,500 books, articles, dissertations, essays, research reports, and other selected documents on all aspects of state legislatures.

Vance Bibliographies

Irregular from Vance Bibliographies, Monticello, IL.

This service has generated hundreds of short, generally unannotated bibliographies since 1978. Most of the bibliographies are the result of competent online bibliographic searches. A title list to this bibliographical series is available from the publisher. Where access to professional online services is lacking, this can be a source of useful very specialized bibliographies.

TITLE INDEX

All titles are indexed here. Governmental bodies, agencies and, with few exceptions, compilers or editors are not indexed.

Associations, publishers and information firms are indexed only if they received special annotation in the text.

A

ABA (AMERICAN BAR ASSOCIATION), 191

ABI/INFORM, 89

ACIR (ADVISORY COMMISSION ON INTERGOVERNMENTAL RELATIONS), 194

Abstract Newsletter: Administration and Management, 90

Abstract Newsletter: Health Care, 90

Abt Electronic Library, 154

Accountant's Index, 96

Accounting Articles, 168

Administration and Society, 101

Administration in Social Work, 101

Administrative Law Review, 101

Administrative Practice Manual, 168

Advisory Commission on Intergovernmental Relations, 156-157, 194

AICPA (AMERICAN INSTITUTE OF CERTIFIED PUBLIC ACCOUNTANTS), 191

Air & Water Pollution Control, 168

All-States Tax Reports, 169

Almanac of American Politics, 3, 205

Almanac of the 50 States, 39

Alternative Press Index, 96

AMA Management Handbook, 59

America Votes, 54

American Academy of Political and Social Science, 102

AMERICAN ACCOUNTING ASSOCIATION, 189

AMERICAN ASSOCIATION OF SMALL CITIES, 190

AMERICAN BAR ASSOCIATION, 191
American Business Law Journal, 102
American City & County, 103
American Demographics, 103
AMERICAN INSTITUTE OF CERTIFIED PUBLIC ACCOUNTANTS, 191
American Journal of Political Science, 103
American Law of Zoning, 169
American Management Association Management Handbook, 59
AMERICAN PLANNING ASSOCIATION, 192
American Political Dictionary, 59
American Political Science Review, 103
American Politics Quarterly, 104
American Public Administration, 214
American Public Opinion Index, 55
AMERICAN PUBLIC WORKS ASSOCIATION, 192
American Reference Books Annual, 1989, 63
American Review of Public Administration, 104
AMERICAN SOCIETY FOR PUBLIC ADMINISTRATION, 193
American Statistical Index, 33
AMERICAN WATER WORKS ASSOCIATION, 193
Andriot, John L., 76
Annals, 102
Annual Register of Grant Support, 65
Annual Survey of Government Finances, 43
Antieau, C.J., 177 ASI, 33
ASSOCIATED PUBLIC-SAFETY COMMUNICATIONS OFFICERS, 190
ASSOCIATION OF GOVERNMENT ACCOUNTANTS, 194

B

Bae, Frank, 221
Bander, Edward J., 69, 221
Baseline Data Report, 104
Bender's Uniform Commercial Code Service, 169
Bibliographic Index, 63
Bibliography of State Bibliographies, 80
Blackwell Encyclopedia of Political Institutions, 59
BLS Data Diskettes, 157
BNA (Bureau of National Affairs), 150, 165
Book of the States, 39, 206
Books in Print, 72
BRS Information Technologies, Inc., 140
Budget of the U.S. Government, 47
Bureau of National Affairs (BNA), 150, 165
Bureaucrat, 104
Business Conditions Digest, 49
Business Information Sources, 68, 214
Business Serials of the U.S. Government, 49
Business Statistics, 52

C

CACI, Inc., 146-147
Caiden, Gerald E., 214
California Journal, 105
Carroll Publishing Company, 8
Catalog of Federal Domestic Assistance, 66, 68
CCH (Commerce Clearing House), 150, 165, 174
CD-ROM; An Annotated Bibliography, 156
CD-ROMs in Print, 156
CENDATA, 145
Census and You, 36
Census Catalog and Guide, 29, 158
Census of Governments, 45

Census of Population and Housing, 40
Census of Population, 40
Charitable Giving and Solicitation, 182
Chitty, Mary Glen, 216
CIS (Congressional Information Service), 16, 33-34, 147
CIS/Index, 74, 147
CIS US Congressional Hearings Index, 16
City Almanac, 105
City and State, 105
City Government Finances, 43
City Hall Digest, 105
Civil Rights Actions, 169
Code of Federal Regulations, 8
Cohen, Morris L., 69, 218
Collective Bargaining Negotiations & Contracts, 169
Columbia Journal of Law and Social Problems, 105
Commerce Clearing House (CCH), 150, 165, 174
Commerce Clearing House, 174
Community Development Journal, 106
Community Resources Directory, 23
Comparative Public Administration, 215
Comparative State Income Tax Guide, 169
Compendium of Government Finances, 45 CompuServe, 140
Computers, Environment and Urban Systems, 106
Condemnation Procedures & Techniques, 169
Condominium Law & Practice, 170
Conference Board, CBDB Data Disk, 156
Congress and the Nation, 17
Congress and the Presidency, 106
Congressional Directory, 5
Congressional District Data Book, 41

Congressional Index, 15, 167
Congressional Information Service (CIS), 16, 33-34, 147
Congressional Quarterly Almanac, 15, 17
Congressional Quarterly, Inc. (CQ), 17
Congressional Quarterly Weekly Report, 15, 106
Congressional Quarterly's Guide to U.S. Elections, 54
Congressional Quarterly's Guide to Congress, 17
Congressional Quarterly's Guide to the Presidency, 17
Congressional Quarterly's Guide to the U.S. Supreme Court, 17
CONGRESSIONAL RECORD ABSTRACTS, 148
Congressional Staff Directory, 6
Congressional Yellow Book, 6, 170
Constitutions of the U.S.: National & State, 170
Consultants and Consulting Organizations Directory, 19
Consumer Product Safety Guide, 170
Contemporary Policy Issues, 106
Cooperative Housing Law & Practice, 170
Cost Accounting Standards Guide, 170
COUNCIL OF STATE GOVERNMENTS, 194, 221
County and City Data Book Data Disk, 156
County and City Data Book, 42, 206
County and City Finance Data on Microcomputer Diskettes, 157
County Executive Directory, 13
County Government Finances, 43
CPI Detailed Report, 50
CQ (Congressional Quarterly, Inc.), 17
CSG Backgrounder, 107
CSI/Federal Index, 96

Cumulative Subject Index to the Monthly Catalog, 78
Current Events Transcripts Service, 16
Current Law Index, 97, 98
Current Municipal Problems, 107, 206
Cutchin, D.A., 217

D

Daniells, Lorna M., 69, 214
Database Directory, 160
DATABASE OF DATABASES, 160
Database, 162
DataPro Directory of On-Line Services, 160
Detailed Population Characteristics, 41
Dialog Information Services, Inc., 137-138, 141
Direct Mail Lists Rates and Data, 26
Directories in Print, 23
Directory of City Policy Officials, 13
Directory of Computer Software, 37
Directory of Computerized Data Files, 37
Directory of Federal Libraries, 71
Directory of Federal Statistical Data Files, 38
Directory of Government Document Collections & Librarians, 71
Directory of Labor Relations, 171
Directory of Microcomputer Data and Software, 103
Directory of Online Databases, 160
Directory of Organizations and Individuals, 20
Directory of Staff Assistants to the Governors, 10
District of Columbia Telephone Directory, 2
DONNELLEY DEMOGRAPHICS, 145
Doyle, Francis A., 221

Dun's Consultants Directory, 20
Dynes, Patrick S., 219

E

EasyNet, 141
Economic Indicators, 50
ECONOMIC LITERATURE INDEX, 91
Economic Report of the President, 47, 207
Economics Sourcebook of Government Statistics, 29
Editorial Research Reports, 107
Educational Administration Abstracts, 90
Employee and Union Member Guide to Labor Law, 171
Employee Benefit Plan Review, 107
Employee Benefits Cases Service, 171
Employee Benefits Compliance Coordinator, 171
Employee Relations Law Journal, 108
Employment and Training Reporter, 171
Employment Practices Guide, 171
Employment Safety & Health Guide, 171
Encyclopedia of Associations, 24, 187
Encyclopedia of Business Information Sources, 215
Encyclopedia of Governmental Advisory Organizations, 7
Encyclopedia of Information Systems and Services, 161
Encyclopedia of Management, 60
Encyclopedia of Public Affairs Information Sources, 215
Encyclopedia of the American Constitution, 60
Environment and Behavior, 108
Environment and Planning C: Government & Policy, 108
Environment Reporter, 172
Equal Employment Opportunity Compliance Manual, 172

Equal Opportunity in Housing, 172

Ethics in Government Reporter, 172

Evaluation and Program Planning, 108

Evaluation Practice, 108

Evaluation Review, 109

Executive Telecom Systems, Inc., 146

Exempt Organizations Reporter, 172

F

Factfinder for the Nation, 30, 158

Facts and Figures on Government Finance, 46, 207

Facts on File Dictionary of Public Administration, 60

Facts on File, 109

Fair Employment Practice Service, 172

Fair Housing-Fair Lending, 172

Faxon Company, 154

Fed in Print, 50, 109

Federal Contracts Report, 173

Federal Database Finder, 37

Federal Election Campaign Financing, 173

Federal Employment Relations Manual, 173

Federal Executive Directory, 7

Federal Information Sources in Health and Medicine, 216

FEDERAL REGISTER ABSTRACTS, 148

Federal Register, 8, 66, 148

Federal Regulatory Directory, 8

Federal Reserve Bulletin, 50, 109

Federal Staff Directory, 9

Federal-State-Local Government Directory, 4

Federal Statistical Data Bases, 38, 157

Federal Statistical Directory, 30

Federal Statistical System 1980 to 1985, 35

Federal Tax Articles, 173

Federal Taxation, 173

Federal Yellow Book, 9

Finances of County Government, 45

Finances of Municipal and Township Governments, 45

Finances of Public School Systems, 45

Finances of Special Districts, 45

Financing State and Local Governments, 48

Forthcoming Books, 72

FOUNDATION DIRECTORY, 67, 68

Foundation Grants Index, 67, 68

From the State Capitals. Public Employee Policy, 110

Fundamentals of Legal Research, 69

FYI...Resources on Local Government, 216

G

Gallup Poll, 56

Gallup Report, 55

GAO Journal, 110

General Periodical Index, 97

General Science Index, 99

General Social and Economic Characteristics, 41

GFOA (GOVERNMENT FINANCE OFFICERS ASSOCIATION), 195-196

Goehlert, Robert U., 222

Government Accountants Journal, 110

Government Contracts Reporter, 174

Government Employee Relations Report, 174

Government Employment, 45

Government Executive, 110

GOVERNMENT FINANCE OFFICERS ASSOCIATION, 195-196

Government Finance Review, 110

Government Organization, 45

Government Product News, 111

Government Programs and Projects Directory, 24

Government Publications Review, 111

Government Reference Serials, 74

Government Reports Announcement & Index, 75

Government Research Centers Directory, 25

Government Union Review, 111

Governmental Finances, 44, 45

Governmental Research Association Directory, 20

GPO MONTHLY CATALOG, 79, 148

GPO PUBLICATIONS REFERENCE FILE, 79, 149

GRA Directory, 20

Group and Organization Studies, 112

Guide to Audits of Local Governments, 48

Guide to Demographic Data Sources, 103

Guide to Grants, 68

Guide to Library Research in Public Administration, 216

Guide to Management Improvement Projects in Local Government, 111

Guide to Municipal Official Statements, 174

Guide to Public Administration, 217

Guide to Reference Books, 63

Guide to Resources and Services, 55, 158

Guide to State Legislative Materials, 81, 175

Guide to Statistical Materials, 31

Guide to the Census of Governments, 46

Guide to the Foundations of Public Administration, 217

Guide to U.S. Government Directories, 76

Guide to U.S. Government Publications, 76

Guide to U.S. Government Statistics, 31

H

H.W. Wilson Company, 144

Handbook of Basic Economic Statistics, 51

Handbook of Human Resources Administration, 61

Handbook of Information Sources and Research Strategies, 218

Handbook of Labor Statistics, 51

Handbook of State Legislative Leaders, 11

Handbook of U.S. Economic and Financial Indicators, 31

Handicapped Americans Report, 175

Harvard Business Review, 112

Harvard Civil Rights - Civil Liberties Law Review, 112

Health Administration: Laws Regulations & Guidelines, 175

Health Care Labor Manual, 175

HEALTH PLANNING & ADMINISTRATION, 90

Historic Documents of 19--, 76

Historical Statistics of the U.S., 40

Holler, Frederick L., 219

Hopkins Technology, 154

Hospital Cost Management, 175

Hospital Literature Index, 91

Housing & Development Reporter, 176

How to Find the Law, 69, 218

HRIN, 146

Huddleston, Mark W., 215

Human Communication Research, 112

Human Resources Abstracts, 91, 93

Human Resources Management, 176

Human Rights Quarterly, 113

I

I.P. Sharp Associates, 147
IAC (Information Access Company), 141
ICMA (INTERNATIONAL CITY MANAGEMENT ASSOCIATION), 14, 197, 216
ICPERS, 149
Index of Economic Articles, 91
Index to Current Urban Documents, 54, 84, 97
Index to Legal Periodicals, 98
Index to Periodical Articles Related to Law, 98
Index to U.S. Government Periodicals, 77, 98, 149
Industrial Relations Guide, 176
Industrial Relations Law Journal, 113
Information Access Company (IAC), 141
Information Sources of Political Science, 219
InfoTrac, 97
Instant Computer Public Employment Relations Search, 149
Inter-University Consortium for Political and Social Research, 55
INTERNATIONAL ASSOCIATION OF ASSESSING OFFICERS, 196
INTERNATIONAL ASSOCIATION OF MUNICIPAL CLERKS, 196
INTERNATIONAL CITY MANAGEMENT ASSOCIATION (ICMA), 14, 197, 216
International Journal of Government Auditing, 113
International Journal of Public Administration, 113
INTERNATIONAL MUNICIPAL SIGNAL ASSOCIATION, 197
Introduction to U.S. Public Documents, 77
Inventory of Data Sources, 159
Investigative Reporters and Editors, Inc., 78
Irregular Serials & Annuals, 73

J

Jacobstein, J. Myron, 69
Journal of Accounting and Public Policy, 114
Journal of Collective Negotiations in the Public Sector, 114
Journal of Community Health, 114
Journal of Economic Literature, 91
Journal of Health and Human Resources Administration, 114
Journal of Health Politics, Policy and Law, 115
Journal of Human Resources, 115
Journal of Management, 115
Journal of Police Science and Administration, 115
Journal of Policy Analysis and Management, 116
Journal of Public Economics, 116
Journal of Public Policy and Marketing, 116
Journal of Research in Crime and Delinquency, 116
Journal of Social Issues, 116
Journal of State Government, 117, 129
Journal of State Taxation, 117
Journal of the American Planning Association, 117
Journal of Urban Affairs, 117
Journal of Volunteer Administration, 117

L

Labor Arbitration Awards, 176
Labor Arbitration Index, 176
Labor Relations Press, 149
Labor Relations Reporter, 177
LABORLAW, 150
Land Use and Zoning Digest, 117
Law and Business Directory of Corporate Counsel, 21
Law and Policy, 118
Law and Society Review, 118
Law of Workman's Compensation, 177
Legal Looseleafs in Print, 167

Legal Resource Index, 98
LegalTrac, 98
Legislative Studies Quarterly, 118
Levitan, Donald, 68
LEXIS, 142, 150
Literary Market Place, 72
Local Government Finances in
  Major County Areas, 44
Local Government in Metropolitan
  Areas, 45
Local Government Law, 177
Local Governments, 90
Locating U.S. Government
  Information, 77

M

M I S (Management Information
  Service) Report, 119
Magazines for Libraries, 133
Major Programs: Bureau of Labor
  Statistics, 32
Management World, 118
Manual of Online Search
  Strategies, 161
Marshall, Marion B., 220
Martin, Daniel W., 217
Martindale-Hubbell Law
  Directory, 21 Marvel, Mark K.,
  219
Mc⌐   ⌐y, Howard E., 220
Mc⌐   ⌐ta Central, 142
Mecklei Corporation, 156
MEDLINE, 91
Meridian Data, Inc., 154
Microsoft Bookshelf: CD ROM
  Reference Library, 155
Microsoft Corp., 154
Minority Consultants and
  Minority-Owned Consulting
  Organizations,
20
Modern Times, 119
Monthly Catalog of U.S.
  Government Publications, 78,
  148
Monthly Checklist of State
  Publications, 81

Monthly Labor Review, 51, 119
Monthly List of GAO Reports, 119
Monthly Products Announcement,
  36
Moody's Municipal and
  Government Manual, 48
Municipal/County Executive
  Directory, 13
Municipal Executive Directory, 13
Municipal Government Reference
  Sources, 85
Municipal Ordinances, 177
Municipal Year Book, 14, 187, 208
Musto, Frederick W., 222

N

Nation's Cities Weekly, 119
NATIONAL ASSOCIATION FOR
  STATE INFORMATION
  SYSTEMS, 198
NATIONAL ASSOCIATION OF
  ATTORNEYS GENERAL, 198
NATIONAL ASSOCIATION OF
  COUNTIES, 198
NATIONAL CENTER FOR STATE
  COURTS, 199
NATIONAL CIVIC LEAGUE, 199
National Civic Review, 120
NATIONAL CONFERENCE OF
  COMMISSIONERS ON
  UNIFORM STATE LAWS, 200
NATIONAL CONFERENCE OF
  STATE LEGISLATURES, 200
National Contract Management
  Journal, 120
National Directory of Corporate
  Public Affairs, 21
National Directory of Newsletters
  and Reporting Services, 110,
  133
National Directory of State
  Agencies, 11
NATIONAL FOUNDATIONS, 67
NATIONAL GOVERNORS
  ASSOCIATION, 200
National Income and Products
  Accounts of the U.S., 52
National Journal, 120

National League of Cities, 94, 201
National Library of Medicine, 90
National Planning Data Corporation, 147
National Public Employment Reporter, 177
National Tax Journal, 120
National Technical Information Service (NTIS), 75
National Trade and Professional Associations of the U.S., 25, 188, 208
Negotiated Employee Benefit Plans, 178
New Directions for Program Evaluation, 121
New Governmental Advisory Organizations, 7
New Research Centers, 70
NEWSEARCH, 151
NewsNet, 143
NEXIS, 142
NLC Washington Report to the Nations Cities, 121
NLRB Case Handling Manual, 178
Northwestern University Law Review, 121
NTIS, 91

O

Occupational Safety & Health Reporter, 178
Online Database Search Services Directory, 161
Online Review, 162
Online, 162
Optical Publishing Directory, 155

P

P-H (Prentice-Hall Law & Business Inc.), 150, 165
PAIS Bulletin, 99
Parish, David W., 82
Parks and Recreation, 121
Pension Plan Guide, 178
Pension Reporter, 178
Personnel Management Abstracts, 92

Personnel Management, 178
Personnel, 180
Policy & Practice Series, 178
Policy Studies Journal, 121
Policy Studies Review, 122
Political Action Committee (PAC), 21
Political Science Quarterly, 122
Politics in America, 9
Polity, 122
Pollution Control Guide, 179
Popular Names of U.S. Government Reports, 79
Prentice-Hall Law & Business Inc. (P-H), 150, 165
Products Liability Reporter, 179
Products Liability, 179
Program Evaluation: An Annotated Bibliography, 219
PROMT, 92
Protection of Abused Victims; State Laws and Decisions, 179
Psychological Abstracts, 92
Public Administration Desk Book, 208
Public Administration Dictionary, 61
Public Administration in American Society: A Guide, 219
Public Administration Quarterly, 122
Public Administration Review, 123
Public Administration: A Guide to the Literature, 220
Public Affairs Information Service, Inc., 99
Public Budgeting and Finance, 123
Public Choice, 123
Public Contract Law Journal, 124
Public Employee Bargaining, 179, 180
Public Finance Quarterly, 124
Public Finance: An Information Sourcebook, 48, 220
Public Health Reports, 124
Public Interest, 124
Public Management, 124

Public Opinion Quarterly, 56
Public Opinion, 56
Public Personnel Management, 125
Public Productivity Review, 125
Public Roads, 125
PUBLIC SECURITIES ASSOCIATION, 202
PUBLIC TECHNOLOGY, INC., 202
Public Utilities Fortnightly, 125
Public Works Manual, 126 Public Works, 126
Publius; The Journal of Federalism, 126

R

R.R. Bowker Company, 154
Real Estate Transactions, 169
Reporter's Handbook, 78
Research Centers Directory, 70
Research Services Directory, 20
Review of Public Personnel Administration, 126
Rock, Mary G., 218
Rouse, John E. Jr., 219
Rural Sociology, 126

S

Safire's Political Dictionary, 61
Sage Public Administration Abstracts, 93
Sage Urban Studies Abstracts, 93
Sales Taxes, 180
School Law Bulletin (Boston), 127
School Law Register, 180
Schwarzkopf, LeRoy C., 74
Science Citation Index, 100
Searching the Law, 69, 221
Securities Regulation & Law Report, 180
Sheehy, Eugene P., 63
Shepard's Law Review Citations, 99
Significant Features of Fiscal Federalism, 46
SilverPlatter Information, Inc., 155
Simpson, Anthony E., 216

SITE II, 146
Social Forces, 127
Social Planning, Policy and Development Abstracts, 93
Social Security Bulletin, 127
Social Science Citation Index, 100
Social Science Index, 99
Social Science Quarterly, 127
Social Service Review, 128
Social Work Research & Abstracts, 94
Social Work, 128
Socio-Economic Planning Sciences, 128
Sociological Abstracts, 93-94
Sources of Information in the Social Sciences, 64
SOUTHERN BUILDING CODE CONGRESS, INTERNATIONAL, 203
Southern California Law Review, 128
SPECIAL LIBRARIES ASSOCIATION, 203
Standard & Poor's Bond Guide, 48
Standard & Poor's Statistical Service, 52
Standard Industrial Classification (SIC), 53
Standard Periodical Directory, 73
Starting and Operating a Business in [State], 181
State Administrative Officials Classified by Function, 11
State and Local Government Political Dictionary, 62
State and Local Government Review, 129
State and Local Government Debt Financing, 181
State and Local Taxes, 181
State and Metropolitan Area Data Book, 42
State Elective Officials and the Legislatures, 12
State Government Finances, 44
State Government News, 129

State Government Reference Publications, 82 State Government Research Checklist, 221
State Government Research Directory, 70
State Government Tax Collections, 44
State Government, 129
State Government: CQ's Guide to Current Issues, 18
State Health Reports, 129
State Legislative Leadership, Committees & Staff, 12, 209
State Legislative Sourcebook, 82
State Legislatures, 129, 222
State Policy Data Book, 41
State Policy Reports, 18, 130
State Tax Action Coordinator, 181
State Tax Guide, 181
State Tax Reports, 181
Statistical Abstract of the U.S., 42, 209
Statistical Policy Handbook, 35
Statistical Reference Index, 34, 54, 55
Statistics Sources, 32
Subject Collections, 70
Subject Compilations of State Laws, 84
Subject Guide to Major U.S. Government Publications, 79
Subject Guide to U.S. Government Reference Sources, 79
Survey of Current Business, 52, 130, 210

T
Tapping the Government Grapevine, 80
Tax Exempt Organizations, 182
Taxable Property Values and Assessment, 45
Taylor's Encyclopedia of Government Officials, 4
Telebase Systems, Inc., 141
Topical Studies, 45

Training and Development Organizations Directory, 22

U
U.S. Budget in Brief, 47
U.S. Bureau of Census, 152
U.S. CONFERENCE OF MAYORS, 203
U.S. Government Manual, 10, 210
U.S. Industrial Outlook, 53
U.S. Law Week, 167
U.S. National Library of Medicine, 90
U.S. Political Science Documents, 95
Ulrich's International Periodical Directory, 73, 133
ULRICH'S, 73
UMI (University Microfilms International), 89, 155
UMI Article Clearinghouse Catalog, 89
Unemployment Insurance Reports, 182
University Microfilms International (UMI), 89, 155
University of Detroit Law Review, 130
Update of the Status of Major Federal Statistical Agencies, 35
UPI NEWS, 151
Urban Affairs Abstracts, 94
Urban Affairs Quarterly, 130
Urban and Social Change Review, 131
Urban Documents Center, 97
URBAN INSTITUTE, 204
Urban Law and Policy, 131
Urban Lawyer, 131
Urban Systems Research and Engineering, Inc., 146-147
Using Government Publications, 80

V
Vance Bibliographies, 222
Vital Speeches of the Day, 16
VU/TEXT, 143

W

Washington Information Directory, 5

Washington Lobbyists & Lawyers Directory, 22

Washington Monthly, 131

Washington Representatives, 22

Washington University Journal of Urban and Contemporary Law, 132

Wasserman, Paul, 215

WATERNET, 194

Ways & Means, 132

West Publishing Company, 144

WESTLAW, 144, 150

Where to Find What, 64

WILSONLINE, 144

Work and Occupations, 132

Work Related Abstracts, 95

Workman's Compensation for Occupational Injuries & Death, 182

World Almanac and Book of Facts, 64, 211

Woy, James, 215

X

X/REGION, 147

Y

Yale Journal on Regulation, 132

Z

Zoning & Land Use Controls, 182

SUBJECT INDEX

Under each subject heading are names of reference works, journals, databases, associations and firms which have special value for that subject. Thus, this subject index can be used independently. A glance at the page numbers will show what part of the *Desk Book* introduces that subject and describes its information tools, journals and services.

ABSTRACTING SERVICES
ABI/INFORM, 89
Accounting Articles [HF 563], 168
Criminal Justice Abstracts, 115-116, 128
Educational Administration Abstracts, 90
Federal Tax Articles [KF 6335], 173
HEALTH PLANNING & ADMINISTRATION, 90
Human Resources Abstracts, 91
Personnel Management Abstracts, 92
PROMT, 92
Psychological Abstracts, 92
Sage Public Administration Abstracts, 93
Sage Urban Studies Abstracts, 93
Social Planning, Policy and Development Abstracts, 93
Social Work Research & Abstracts, 94
Sociological Abstracts, 94
Statistical Abstract of the United States, 42, 209
United States Political Science Documents, 95
Urban Affairs Abstracts, 94
Work Related Abstracts, 95
ACCOUNTING
Accounting Articles [HF 563], 168

AMERICAN ACCOUNTING
ASSOCIATION, 189
AICPA, 191
An Inventory of Data Sources,
159
ASSOCIATION OF
GOVERNMENT
ACCOUNTANTS, 194
Business Information Sources,
68, 214
Cost Accounting Standards
Guide [KF 846.5], 171
GOVERNMENT FINANCE
OFFICERS ASSOCIATION,
195
Guide to Audits of Local
Governments, 48
Tax Exempt Organizations [KF
6449], 172, 182

ACCOUNTING (JOURNALS)
GAO Journal, 110
Government Accountants
Journal, 110
International Journal of
Government Auditing, 113
Journal of Accounting and
Public Policy, 114
Monthly List of GAO Reports,
119
National Tax Journal, 120

ADMINISTRATION (JOURNALS)
Administration and
Management, 90
Administrative Science
Quarterly, 102
American Journal of Political
Science, 103
American Political Science
Review, 103
American Review of Public
Administration, 104
Bureaucrat, 104
Government Executive, 110
Group and Organization
Studies, 112
Human Communication
Research, 112

International Journal of Public
Administration, 113
Journal of Management, 115
Public Administration
Quarterly, 122
Public Administration Review,
123
Publius, 126

**ADMINISTRATIVE LAW
(JOURNALS)**
Administrative Law Review, 101
CSI/Federal Index, 96
Federal Register, 96
Law and Policy, 118
National Journal, 120
Yale Journal on Regulation,
132

ALTERNATIVE STUDIES
Alternative Press Index, 96
Ways & Means, 132

AMBASSADORS
Congressional Directory, 5
Washington Information
Directory, 5

ARMED FORCES (see MILITARY)

ASSISTANCE, GOVERNMENT
Catalog of Federal Domestic
Assistance, 66
Federal Register, 66
Government Programs and
Projects Directory, 24
Government Research Centers
Directory, 25
State Policy Data Book, 41
Unemployment Insurance
Reports [KF 3673], 182

ASSOCIATIONS
Directory of Organizations and
Individuals, 20
Encyclopedia of Associations,
24, 187
Federal-State-Local
Government Directory, 4
Municipal Year Book, 14, 187,
208

National Directory of State Agencies, 11
National Trade and Professional Associations, 25, 188, 208

ATLASES
Congressional Directory, 5
Congressional Yellow Book, 6
Locating U.S. Government Information, 77
State Government Reference Publications, 82
Taylor's Encyclopedia of Government Officials, 4

AUDIOVISUAL GUIDES
Locating U.S. Government Information, 77
State Government Reference Publications, 82

BANKING
Fed in Print, 109
Federal Reserve Bulletin, 50, 109
National Tax Journal, 120
Public Choice, 123
Standard & Poor's Statistical Service, 52

BENEFITS, GOVERNMENT (see also ASSISTANCE)
Law of Workman's Compensation [KF 3613], 177
Public Employee Bargaining [KF 3409], 179
Public Personnel Administration [KF 3580], 180

BIBLIOGRAPHIES, SOURCES (see also ABSTRACTING SERVICES, INDEXING SERVICES)
American Reference Books Annual, 63
Bibliographic Index, 63
Bibliography of State Bibliographies, 80
FYI...; Resources on Local Government, 216
Guide to Reference Books, 63

Locating U.S. Government Information, 77
Recent Publications on Governmental Problems, 221
State Government Reference Publications, 82
State Government Research Checklist, 221
State Legislative Sourcebook, 82
Subject Compilations of State Laws, 84
Subject Guide to Major U.S. Government Publications, 79
Subject Guide to U.S. Government Reference Sources, 79
Vance Bibliographies, 222

BIOGRAPHIES
Congressional Directory, 5
Congressional Index, 15
CQ's Guide to Congress, 17
CQ's Guide to the Presidency, 17
CQ's Guide to the U.S. Supreme Court, 17
Congressional Staff Directory, 6
Congressional Yellow Book, 6
Facts on File Dictionary of Public Administration, 60
Federal Staff Directory, 9
Federal-State-Local Government Directory, 4
Handbook of State Legislative Leaders, 11
Politics in America, 9

BONDS, GOVERNMENT
Moody's Municipal and Government Manual, 48
Public Finance: An Information Sourcebook, 48
PUBLIC SECURITIES ASSOCIATION, 202
Standard & Poor's Bond Guide, 48

BONDS, MUNICIPAL
City and State, 105
Moody's Municipal and
Government Manual, 48
Public Finance: An Information
Sourcebook, 48
Standard & Poor's Bond Guide,
48
State and Local Government
Debt Financing [KF 6724],
181

BUDGETING
Budget of the U.S.
Government, 47
CQ Weekly Report, 15, 106
State and Local Government
Debt Financing [KF 6724],
181
United States Budget in Brief,
47

BUDGETING (JOURNALS)
Government Finance Review,
110
Public Budgeting and Finance,
123

**BUSINESS (see also ECONOMIC
INDICATORS, MANAGEMENT)**
ABI/INFORM, 89
Business Conditions Digest, 49
Business Information Sources,
68, 214
Business Serials of the U.S.
Government, 49
CPI Detailed Report, 50
Economic Indicators, 50
Encyclopedia of Business
Information Sources, 215
Federal Reserve Bulletin, 50
Handbook of Basic Economic
Statistics, 51
Handbook of Labor Statistics,
51
Monthly Labor Review, 51
NEWSEARCH, 151
PROMPT, 92
Standard & Poor's Statistical
Service, 52

Starting and Operating a
Business in [State] [KFM
2634], 181
Survey of Current Business,
52, 210
U.S. Industrial Outlook, 53
Survey of Current Business,
130

BUSINESS (JOURNALS)
Business Conditions Digest, 49
CPI Detailed Report, 50
Economic Indicators, 50
Employee Benefit Plan Review,
107
Federal Reserve Bulletin, 50
Harvard Business Review, 112
Journal of Public Policy and
Marketing, 116
Monthly Labor Review, 51
Public Choice, 123
State Government, 129
Survey of Current Business,
52, 210

BUSINESS LAW
Bender's Uniform Commercial
Code Service [KF 885], 169
Starting and Operating a
Business in [State] [KFM
2634], 181

BUSINESS LAW (JOURNALS)
American Business Law
Journal, 102
Bureaucrat, 104
Journal of Public Policy and
Marketing, 116
National Contract Management
Journal, 120
National Tax Journal, 120
Public Contract Law Journal,
124
Public Personnel Management,
125

CAMPAIGN FINANCE
Almanac of American Politics,
3, 205
Handbook of State Legislative
Leaders, 11

National Directory of Corporate
Public Affairs, 21
Politics in America, 9

CAMPAIGNS, POLITICAL
CQ Almanac, 15
CQ Weekly Report, 15, 106
CQ's Guide to U.S. Elections,
54

CASE LAW
LEXIS, 150
WESTLAW, 150

CD-ROM
Abt Electronic Library (617)
661-1300, 154
CD-ROM; An Annotated
Bibliography, 156
CD-ROMs in Print, 156
Census Catalog and Guide, 158
Hopkins Technology
(612)931-9376), 154
Meckler Corporation (203)
226-6967, 156
Meridian Data, Inc.
(408)476-5858, 154
R.R. Bowker (800) 257-7894,
154
SilverPlatter Information, Inc.
(617) 239-0306, 155
The Faxon Company (800)
225-6055, 154
Optical Publishing Directory,
155
University Microfilms
International (800)
521-3044, 155

CENSUS
CENDATA, 145
Census and You, 36
Census Catalog and Guide, 29
Census of Population and
Housing, 40
Congressional District Data
Book, 41
County and City Data Book,
42, 206
Detailed Population
Characteristics, 41

Factfinder for the Nation, 30
Federal Statistical Data Bases,
157
General Social and Economic
Characteristics, 41
Historical Statistics of the
United States, 40
Monthly Products
Announcement, 36
State and Metropolitan Area
Data Book, 42
State Data Centers, 158
Statistical Abstract of the
United States, 42, 209

CHILD WELFARE
Protection of Abused Victims
[KF 9320], 179

CIVIL RIGHTS
Civil Rights Actions [KF 4749],
169
Employment Practices Guide
[KF 3464], 171
EEO Compliance Manual [KF
3464], 172
Equal Opportunity in Housing
[KF 5740], 172
Fair Employment Practice
Service [KF 3314], 172
Fair Housing-Fair Lending [KF
5740], 172
Handicapped Americans Report
[KF 480], 175
Labor Relations Reporter [KF
3314], 177
Protection of Abused Victims
[KF 9320], 179

CIVIL RIGHTS (JOURNALS)
Harvard Civil Rights/Civil
Liberties Law Review, 112
Human Rights Quarterly, 113
Social Science Quarterly, 127

COLLECTIVE BARGAINING
Collective Bargaining
Negotiations & Contracts [KF
3408], 169
Directory of Labor Relations
[KF 3421], 171

Labor Arbitration Awards [KF 9085], 176

Labor Arbitration Index [KF 3421.5], 176

NLRB Case Handling Manual [KF 3372], 178

Public Employee Bargaining [KF 3409], 179, 180

COMMUNICATIONS

ASSOCIATED PUBLIC-SAFETY COMMUNICATIONS OFFICERS, 190

INTERNATIONAL MUNICIPAL SIGNAL ASSOCIATION, 197

COMMUNITY RESOURCES

Community Resources Directory, 23

COMPUTER APPLICATIONS (JOURNALS)

Computers, Environment and Urban Systems, 106

M I S (Management Information Service) Report, 119

Management World, 118

COMPUTER DATABASES (see DATA SERVICES, ONLINE SERVICES)

CONGRESS (see also LEGISLATION, POLITICAL SCIENCE)

Almanac of American Politics, 3, 205

CIS/Index, 74, 147

Congress and the Nation, 17

Congressional Directory, 5

Congressional Index, 15, 167

CQ Almanac, 15

CQ's Guide to Congress, 17

CQ's Guide to U.S. Elections, 54

CONGRESSIONAL RECORD ABSTRACTS, 148

Congressional Staff Directory, 6

Congressional Yellow Book, 6, 170

Current Events Transcripts Service, 16

Federal Executive Directory, 7

Federal-State-Local Government Directory, 4

Politics in America, 9

Taylor's Encyclopedia of Government Officials, 4

United States Government Manual, 10, 210

Washington Information Directory, 5

CONGRESS (JOURNALS)

Congress and the Presidency, 106

CQ Weekly Report, 15, 106

Editorial Research Reports, 107

Legislative Studies Quarterly, 118

Nation's Cities Weekly, 119

National Journal, 120

CONGRESSIONAL STAFF

Congressional Staff Directory, 6

Congressional Yellow Book, 170

CONSTITUTIONS

Constitutions of the U.S. [KF 4530], 170

Encyclopedia of the American Constitution, 60

NATIONAL CIVIC LEAGUE, 199

CONSTRUCTION

AMERICAN PUBLIC WORKS ASSOCIATION, 192

Government Reports Announcement & Index, 75

Index to U.S. Government Periodicals, 77, 98, 149

NTIS, 91

SOUTHERN BUILDING CODE CONGRESS, INTERNATIONAL, 203

CONSULTANTS

Consultants and Consulting Organizations Directory, 19

Directory of Organizations and Individuals, 20

Dun's Consultants Directory, 20

Encyclopedia of Information Systems and Services, 161

Minority Consultants, 20

Online Database Search Services Directory, 161

Research Services Directory, 20

Washington Representatives, 22

CONSUMER AFFAIRS

American Demographics, 103

Consumer Product Safety Guide [KF 1606], 170

FEDERAL REGISTER ABSTRACTS, 148

NEWSEARCH, 151

Products Liability Reporter [KF 1296], 179

Products Liability [KF 1296], 179

Public Choice, 123

CONTRACTS AND CONTRACTING

Government Programs and Projects Directory, 24

Government Research Centers Directory, 25

Federal Contracts Report [KF 846], 173

FEDERAL REGISTER ABSTRACTS, 148

Government Contracts Reporter [KF 846], 174

CORRECTIONS (see CRIMINAL JUSTICE, LAW ENFORCEMENT)

COST OF LIVING (see ECONOMIC INDICATORS)

COURTS (see also CRIMINAL JUSTICE, LAW, LAW ENFORCEMENT)

LEXIS, 150

Martindale-Hubbell Law Directory, 21

NATIONAL CENTER FOR STATE COURTS, 199

United States Law Week [KF 105], 167

WESTLAW, 150

CRIMINAL JUSTICE (see also LAW ENFORCEMENT)

Abt Electronic Library (617) 661-1300, 154

Census of Governments, 45

Criminal Justice Abstracts, 115-116, 128

NATIONAL ASSOCIATION OF ATTORNEYS GENERAL, 198

NATIONAL CENTER FOR STATE COURTS, 199

Protection of Abused Victims [KF 9320], 179

State Policy Data Book, 41

Statistical Abstract of the United States, 42, 209

CRIMINAL JUSTICE (JOURNALS)

Evaluation Review, 109

Journal of Police Science and Administration, 115

Journal of Research in Crime and Delinquency, 116

Journal of Social Issues, 116

Law & Society Review, 117

Law and Policy, 118

Northwestern University Law Review, 121

Social Forces, 127

Southern California Law Review, 128

DATA SERVICES

ACIR, 156, 189

Baseline Data Report, 104

CENDATA, 145

Census Catalog and Guide, 158

County and City Finance Data, 157

County and City Data Book, 156

Directory of Computer Software, 37

Directory of Computerized Data Files, 37

Federal Database Finder, 37

Federal Information Sources in Health and Medicine, 216

Federal Statistical Data Bases, 38, 157

Guide to Resources and Services, 55

Hopkins Technology (612)931-9376), 154

Inter-University Consortium, 158

Monthly Products Announcement, 36

State Data Centers, 158

DEMOGRAPHIC DATA

Almanac of American Politics, 3, 205

Almanac of the 50 States, 39

American Demographics, 103

CACI, Inc. (800) 292-2224, 146

Census Catalog and Guide, 158

Census of Population and Housing, 40

Congressional District Data Book, 41

County and City Data Book, 42, 156, 206

Detailed Population Characteristics, 41

Encyclopedia of Information Systems and Services, 161

Factfinder for the Nation, 158

Federal Statistical Data Bases, 157

General Social and Economic Characteristics, 41

Historical Statistics of the United States, 40

I.P. Sharp Associates (416) 364-5361, 147

National Planning Data (202) 265-7685, 147

State and Metropolitan Area Data Book, 42

State Data Centers, 158

State Policy Data Book, 41

Statistical Abstract of the United States, 42, 209

Urban Systems Research (202) 293-3240, 147

DEMOGRAPHIC DATABASES

CENDATA, 145

County and City Data Book Data Disk, 156

DataPro Directory of On-Line Services, 160

DONNELLEY DEMOGRAPHICS, 145

SITE II, 146

X/REGION, 147

DEMOGRAPHICS

American Demographics, 103

Guide to Demographic Data Sources, 103

Social Work, 128

DEPARTMENTS AND AGENCIES, GOVERNMENTAL

American Statistical Index, 33

Congressional Directory, 5

CQ Almanac, 15

CQ Weekly Report, 15

Congressional Staff Directory, 6

Congressional Yellow Book, 6

County Executive Directory, 13

Directory of Staff Assistants to the Governors, 10

Federal Executive Directory, 7

Federal Regulatory Directory, 8

Federal Staff Directory, 9

Federal Statistical Directory, 30

Federal Yellow Book, 9

Federal-State-Local Government Directory, 4

Government Programs and Projects Directory, 24

Government Research Centers Directory, 25

Housing & Development Reporter [KF 5726], 176

Municipal Executive Directory, 13

Municipal Year Book, 14, 187, 208

Municipal/County Executive Directory, 13

National Directory of State Agencies, 11

State Administrative Officials, 11

State Government Research Directory, 70

State Legislative Leadership, 12, 209

United States Government Manual, 10, 210

Washington Information Directory, 5

DICTIONARIES

American Political Dictionary, 59

Blackwell Encyclopedia of Political Institutions, 59

Encyclopedia of Management, 60

Encyclopedia of the American Constitution, 60

Facts on File Dictionary of Public Administration, 60

Guide to Public Administration, 217

Public Administration Dictionary, 61

Safire's Political Dictionary, 61

State and Local Government Political Dictionary, 62

DIPLOMATS (see AMBASSADORS, EMBASSIES)

DIRECTORIES

Almanac of American Politics, 3, 205

Catalog of Federal Domestic Assistance, 66

Community Resources Directory, 23

Congressional Directory, 5

Congressional Staff Directory, 6

Congressional Yellow Book, 6, 170

Consultants and Consulting Organizations Directory, 19

County Executive Directory, 13

Directories in Print, 23

Directory of City Policy Officials, 13

Directory of Federal Libraries, 71

Directory of Organizations and Individuals, 20

Directory of Staff Assistants to the Governors, 10

Dun's Consultants Directory, 20

Encyclopedia of Associations, 24, 187

Encyclopedia of Governmental Advisory Organizations, 7

Federal Executive Directory, 7

Federal Regulatory Directory, 8

Federal Staff Directory, 9

Federal Statistical Directory, 30

Federal Yellow Book, 9

Federal-State-Local Government Directory, 4

Foundation Directory, 67

FOUNDATION GRANTS INDEX, 68

Government Programs and Projects Directory, 24

Government Research Centers Directory, 25

Guide to U.S. Government Directories, 76

Handbook of State Legislative Leaders, 11

Housing & Development Reporter [KF 5726], 176

Law and Business Directory of Corporate Counsel, 21

Literary Market Place, 72

Martindale-Hubbell Law Directory, 21

Minority Consultants, 20

Municipal Executive Directory, 13

Municipal Year Book, 14, 187, 208

National Directory of Corporate Public Affairs, 21

National Directory of State Agencies, 11

NATIONAL FOUNDATIONS, 67

National Trade and
Professional Associations,
25, 188, 208
Research Centers Directory, 70
Research Services Directory, 20
Standard Periodical Directory,
73
State Administrative Officials,
11
State Elective Officials and the
Legislatures, 12
State Government Research
Directory, 70
State Legislative Leadership,
12, 209
Subject Collections, 70
Taylor's Encyclopedia of
Government Officials, 4
Training and Development
Organizations Directory, 22
Ulrich's International
Periodicals Directory, 73
United States Government
Manual, 10, 210
Washington Information
Directory, 5
Washington Lobbyists &
Lawyers Directory, 22
Washington Representatives, 22

DISABLED
ACIR, 189
Handicapped Americans
Report [KF 480], 175

**DISCRIMINATION (see CIVIL
RIGHTS)**

ECONOMIC INDICATORS
BLS Data Diskettes, 157
Business Conditions Digest, 49
CPI Detailed Report, 50
Economic Indicators, 50
Economic Report of the
President, 47, 207
Federal Reserve Bulletin, 50
Handbook of Basic Economic
Statistics, 51
Handbook of Labor Statistics,
51

Handbook of U.S. Economic
and Financial Indicators, 31
Human Resources
Management [KF 3455], 176
Major Programs: Bureau of
Labor Statistics, 32
Policy & Practice Series [KF
3812 or KF 3788], 178
Standard & Poor's Statistical
Service, 52
Survey of Current Business,
52, 130, 210

ECONOMICS (JOURNALS)
ECONOMIC LITERATURE
INDEX, 91
Fed in Print, 109
Federal Reserve Bulletin, 109
Index of Economic Articles, 91
Journal of Economic
Literature, 91
Journal of Human Resources,
Education, Manpower, 115
Journal of Public Economics,
116
Monthly Labor Review, 119
Political Science Quarterly, 122
Public Budgeting and Finance,
123
Public Choice, 123
Public Finance Quarterly, 124
Public Productivity Review, 125
Socio-Economic Planning
Sciences, 128
Urban and Social Change
Review, 131

EDUCATION
Finances of Public School
Systems, 45
General Social and Economic
Characteristics, 41
Government Reports
Announcement & Index, 75
Governmental Finances, 45
Public Employee Bargaining
[KF 3409], 179, 180
School Law Register [KF 4115],
180

State Policy Data Book, 41

EDUCATION (JOURNALS)
Administrative Science
Quarterly, 102
Educational Administration
Abstracts, 90
Journal of Human Resources,
Education, Manpower, 115
Public Personnel Management,
125
School Law Bulletin (Boston),
127
Social Forces, 127
Socio-Economic Planning
Sciences, 128

**ELECTED OFFICIALS (see
GOVERNMENT OFFICIALS)**

ELECTIONS
Almanac of American Politics,
3, 205
America Votes, 54
Book of the States, 39, 206
CQ Almanac, 15
CQ's Guide to U.S. Elections,
54
Congressional Staff Directory, 6
Ethics in Government Reporter
[KF 4568], 172
Federal Election Campaign
Financing [KF 4920], 173
Guide to Resources and
Services, 158
Politics in America, 9
Statistical Abstract of the
United States, 42, 209

EMBASSIES
Congressional Directory, 5
Washington Information
Directory, 5

EMPLOYEE BENEFITS
Employee Benefits Cases
Service [KF 3315], 171
Negotiated Employee Benefit
Plans [KF 3510], 178
Pension Plan Guide [KF 736],
178

Pension Reporter [KF 3510],
178

**EMPLOYMENT (see also
PERSONNEL MANAGEMENT)**
BLS Data Diskettes, 157
Economic Report of the
President, 47, 207
Employment and Training
Reporter [KF 3775], 171
Employment Practices Guide
[KF 3464], 171
Employment Safety & Health
Guide [KF 3568.4], 171
EEO Compliance Manual [KF
3464], 172
Fair Employment Practice
Service [KF 3314], 172
Federal Employment Relations
Manual [KF 3409], 173
Government Employee
Relations Report [KF 3580],
174
Government Employment, 45
Handbook of Labor Statistics,
51
HRIN, 146
ICPERS, 149
LABORLAW, 150
Law of Workman's
Compensation [KF 3613], 177
Occupational Safety & Health
Reporter [KF 3568], 178
Public Employee Bargaining
[KF 3409], 179, 180
Public Personnel
Administration [KF 3580],
180
Unemployment Insurance
Reports [KF 3673], 182
Workman's Compensation [KF
3613], 182

EMPLOYMENT (JOURNALS)
Columbia Journal of Law and
Social Problems, 105
Human Resources Abstracts,
91
Journal of Human Resources,
Education, Manpower, 115

Monthly Labor Review, 119
Personnel Management
Abstracts, 92
University of Detroit Law
Review, 130
Work and Occupations, 132

**ENCYCLOPEDIAS (see
DICTIONARIES)**

ENGINEERING
Air & Water Pollution Control
[KF 3775], 168
BNA (Bureau of National
Affairs) (202)452-7889, 183
Environment Reporter [KF
3775], 172
Government Reports
Announcement & Index, 75
Pollution Control Guide [KF
3775], 179

ENGINEERING (JOURNALS)
American City & County, 103
Government Product News, 111
Public Roads, 125
Public Utilities Fortnightly, 125
Public Works, 126

ENVIRONMENT
Air & Water Pollution Control
[KF 3775], 168
BNA (Bureau of National
Affairs) (202)452-7889, 183
Environment Reporter [KF
3775], 172
Pollution Control Guide [KF
3775], 179
Zoning & Land Use Controls
[KF 5698], 183

ENVIRONMENT (JOURNALS)
Computers, Environment and
Urban Systems, 106
Environment and Behavior, 108
Environment and Planning, 108
Journal of Urban Affairs, 117
Public Health Reports, 124
Public Works, 126

ETHICS
Bureaucrat, 104

Ethics in Government Reporter
[KF 4568], 172

EVALUATION
Program Evaluation, 219

EVALUATION (JOURNALS)
Evaluation and Program
Planning, 108
Evaluation Practice, 108
Evaluation Review, 109
Public Budgeting and Finance,
123
Socio-Economic Planning
Sciences, 128

EXECUTIVE BRANCH, FEDERAL
Almanac of American Politics,
3, 205
Congressional Directory, 5
CQ Almanac, 15
CQ Weekly Report, 15
CQ's Guide to the Presidency,
17
CQ's Guide to U.S. Elections,
54
Current Events Transcripts
Service, 16
Federal Executive Directory, 7
Federal Regulatory Directory, 8
Federal Staff Directory, 9
Federal Yellow Book, 9
National Journal, 120
Taylor's Encyclopedia of
Government Officials, 4
United States Government
Manual, 10, 210

EXECUTIVE BRANCH, STATE
Almanac of American Politics,
3, 205
CQ's Guide to U.S. Elections,
54
Directory of Staff Assistants to
the Governors, 10
Federal-State-Local
Government Directory, 4
NATIONAL GOVERNORS
ASSOCIATION, 200
State Elective Officials and the
Legislatures, 12

EXPENDITURES
Annual Survey of Government Finances, 43
Budget of the U.S. Government, 47
City Government Finances, 43
County Government Finances, 43
Federal Contracts Report [KF 846], 173
Government Contracts Reporter [KF 846], 174
Governmental Finances, 44
Local Government Finances in Major County Areas, 44
Public Finance: An Information Sourcebook, 220
Significant Features of Fiscal Federalism, 46
State Government Finances, 44

FEDERAL AGENCIES (see DEPARTMENTS AND AGENCIES, GOVERNMENTAL)

FEDERAL EMPLOYMENT
Federal Employment Relations Manual [KF 3409], 173
Government Employee Relations Report [KF 3580], 174
Government Employment, 45
National Public Employment Reporter [KF 3580], 177
Public Employee Bargaining [KF 3409], 179, 180
Public Personnel Administration [KF 3580], 180

FEDERAL GOVERNMENT
Almanac of American Politics, 3, 205
Budget of the U.S. Government, 47
Congress and the Nation, 17
Congressional Directory, 5
Congressional Index, 15
CQ Almanac, 15
CQ Weekly Report, 15
CQ's Guide to Congress, 17
CQ's Guide to the Presidency, 17
Congressional Staff Directory, 6
Congressional Yellow Book, 6
Current Events Transcripts Service, 16
Directory of Federal Libraries, 71
Encyclopedia of Governmental Advisory Organizations, 7
Federal Executive Directory, 7
Federal Regulatory Directory, 8
Federal Staff Directory, 9
Federal Yellow Book, 9
Federal-State-Local Government Directory, 4
Government Programs and Projects Directory, 24
Government Research Centers Directory, 25
Politics in America, 9
Taylor's Encyclopedia of Government Officials, 4
United States Budget in Brief, 47
United States Government Manual, 10, 210
Washington Information Directory, 5

FEDERAL INFORMATION CENTERS
Washington Information Directory, 5

FEDERAL RESERVE BANKS (see BANKING)

FEDERALISM
ACIR, 189
Financing State and Local Governments, 48
State Government: CQ's Guide, 18

FEDERALISM (JOURNALS)
Problem-Solving Information, 90
CSG Backgrounder, 107

Intergovernmental Perspective, 194

Journal of State Government, 117

Publius, 126

State Government, 129

Ways & Means, 132

FINANCE

ACIR, 189

AMA Management Handbook, 59

Annual Survey of Government Finances, 43-44

Business Conditions Digest, 49

CPI Detailed Report, 50

Economic Indicators, 50

Economic Report of the President, 47, 207

Economic Sourcebook of Government Statistics, 29-30

Guide to Municipal Official Statements [KF 5315], 174

Handbook of Basic Economic Statistics, 51

Historical Statistics of the United States, 40

Standard & Poor's Bond Guide, 48

Standard & Poor's Statistical Service, 52

FINANCE (JOURNALS)

City and State, 105

Fed in Print, 109

Federal Reserve Bulletin, 109

GAO Journal, 110

Government Accountants Journal, 110

Government Finance Review, 110

Journal of State Taxation, 117

Public Budgeting and Finance, 123

Public Finance Quarterly, 124

Public Utilities Fortnightly, 125

Survey of Current Business, 130

FINANCIAL MANAGEMENT

ACIR, 189

ASSOCIATION OF GOVERNMENT ACCOUNTANTS, 194

Financing State and Local Governments, 48

GOVERNMENT FINANCE OFFICERS ASSOCIATION, 195

Guide to Municipal Official Statements [KF 5315], 174

Public Finance: An Information Sourcebook, 220

Significant Features of Fiscal Federalism, 46

State and Local Government Debt Financing [KF 6724], 181

FINANCIAL STATISTICS (see STATISTICS, ECONOMIC INDICATORS)

FOUNDATIONS

Annual Register of Grant Support, 65

Foundation Directory, 67

FOUNDATION GRANTS INDEX, 68

NATIONAL FOUNDATIONS, 67

GOVERNMENT ADVISORY COMMITTEES

Encyclopedia of Governmental Advisory Organizations, 7

United States Government Manual, 10, 210

GOVERNMENT CONTRACTS (see CONTRACTS AND CONTRACTING)

GOVERNMENT OFFICIALS

Almanac of American Politics, 3, 205

Congress and the Nation, 17

Congressional Directory, 5

Congressional Index, 15

CQ Almanac, 15

CQ Weekly Report, 15

CQ's Guide to Congress, 17

CQ's Guide to the Presidency, 17

Congressional Staff Directory, 6

Congressional Yellow Book, 6

County Executive Directory, 13

Current Events Transcripts Service, 16

Directory of City Policy Officials, 13

Directory of Staff Assistants to the Governors, 10

Encyclopedia of Governmental Advisory Organizations, 7

Federal Executive Directory, 7

Federal Regulatory Directory, 8

Federal Staff Directory, 9

Federal Yellow Book, 9

Federal-State-Local Government Directory, 4

Handbook of State Legislative Leaders, 11

Municipal Executive Directory, 13

Municipal Year Book, 14, 187, 208

Municipal/County Executive Directory, 13

National Directory of State Agencies, 11

Politics in America, 9

State Administrative Officials, 11

State Elective Officials and the Legislatures, 12

State Legislative Leadership, 12, 209

Taylor's Encyclopedia of Government Officials, 4

United States Government Manual, 10, 210

Vital Speeches of the Day, 16

Washington Information Directory, 5

GOVERNMENT OFFICIALS, PHOTOGRAPHS

Congressional Yellow Book, 6

Handbook of State Legislative Leaders, 11

Politics in America, 9

Taylor's Encyclopedia of Government Officials, 4

GOVERNMENT PRINTING OFFICE

Cumulative Subject Index to the Monthly Catalog, 79

GPO MONTHLY CATALOG, 79

GPO PUBLICATIONS REFERENCE FILE, 79

Introduction to U.S. Public Documents, 77

Monthly Catalog of Government Publications, 78

GOVERNMENT PUBLICATIONS

Bibliography of State Bibliographies, 80

CIS/Index, 74, 147

CSI Federal Index, 96

Cumulative Subject Index to the Monthly Catalog, 79

Directory of Government Document Collections & Librarians, 71

Government Reference Serials, 74

Government Reports Announcement & Index, 75

GPO MONTHLY CATALOG, 79, 148

GPO PUBLICATIONS REFERENCE FILE, 79

Guide to State Legislative Materials, 81

Guide to U.S. Government Directories, 76

Guide to U.S. Government Publications, 76

Historic Documents of 19--, 76

Index to Current Urban Documents, 84

Index to U.S. Government Periodicals, 77, 98, 149

Introduction to U.S. Public Documents, 77

Locating U.S. Government Information, 77

Monthly Catalog of
Government Publications, 78
Monthly Checklist of State
Publications, 81
Monthly List of GAO Reports,
119
Municipal Government
Reference Sources, 85
Popular Names of U.S.
Government Reports, 79
Recent Publications on
Governmental Problems, 221
Reporter's Handbook, 78
State Government Reference
Publications, 82
State Government Research
Checklist, 221
State Legislative Sourcebook,
82

**GOVERNMENT PUBLICATIONS
(JOURNALS)**
Fed in Print, 109
Government Publications
Review, 111

**GOVERNMENT PUBLICATIONS,
AIDS AND GUIDES**
Bibliography of State
Bibliographies, 80
Business Serials of the U.S.
Government, 49
Census and You, 36
Census Catalog and Guide, 29
CIS/INDEX, 147
Government Reference Serials,
74
GPO MONTHLY CATALOG, 148
GPO PUBLICATIONS
REFERENCE FILE, 149
Guide to State Legislative
Materials, 81
Guide to U.S. Government
Directories, 76
Guide to U.S. Government
Publications, 76
Guide to U.S. Government
Statistics, 31
Introduction to U.S. Public
Documents, 77

Locating U.S. Government
Information, 77
Monthly Checklist of State
Publications, 81
Monthly Products
Announcement, 36
Municipal Government
Reference Sources, 85
Popular Names of U.S.
Government Reports, 79
State Government Reference
Publications, 82
State Legislative Sourcebook,
82
Subject Guide to Major U.S.
Government Publications, 79
Subject Guide to U.S.
Government Reference
Sources, 79
Tapping the Government
Grapevine, 80
Using Government
Publications, 80

**GOVERNMENT PUBLICATIONS,
INDEXES AND ABSTRACTS**
CIS/Index, 74
GPO MONTHLY CATALOG, 79
GPO PUBLICATIONS
REFERENCE FILE, 79
Index to Current Urban
Documents, 84
Index to U.S. Government
Periodicals, 77, 98, 149
Monthly Catalog of
Government Publications, 78

**GOVERNMENT REGULATIONS
(see also REGULATION)**
CIS/INDEX, 147
FEDERAL REGISTER
ABSTRACTS, 148
LEXIS, 150
WESTLAW, 150

GRANTS
Annual Register of Grant
Support, 65
Catalog of Federal Domestic
Assistance, 66

Federal Register, 66
Foundation Directory, 67
FOUNDATION GRANTS INDEX, 68
Government Programs and Projects Directory, 24
Guide to Grants: Governmental and Nongovernmental, 68
NATIONAL FOUNDATIONS, 67

HANDBOOKS
AMA Management Handbook, 59
Handbook of Human Resources Administration, 61
How to Find the Law, 218
Locating U.S. Government Information, 77
Searching the Law, 221

HEALTH
Air & Water Pollution Control [KF 3775], 168
Aspen Publishers (800)638-8437, 183
Employment Safety & Health Guide [KF 3568.4], 171
Federal Information Sources in Health and Medicine, 216
Health Administration: Laws Regulations [KF 3821], 175
Health Care Labor Manual [KF 3580], 175
National Health Publishing (800)446-2221, 183
Occupational Safety & Health Reporter [KF 3568], 178
Pollution Control Guide [KF 3775], 179
Products Liability Reporter [KF 1296], 179
Products Liability [KF 1296], 179
State Policy Data Book, 41
Workman's Compensation [KF 3613], 182

HEALTH ADMINISTRATION
Health Care Labor Manual [KF 3580], 175

HEALTH PLANNING & ADMINISTRATION, 90
Hospital Cost Management [RA 971], 175

HEALTH CARE
Government Reports Announcement & Index, 75
HEALTH PLANNING & ADMINISTRATION, 90
Hospital Literature Index, 91
MEDLINE, 91

HEALTH CARE (JOURNALS)
Health Care, 90
Journal of Community Health, 114
Journal of Health and Human Resources Administration, 114
Journal of Health Politics, Policy and Law, 115
Public Health Reports, 124
Socio-Economic Planning Sciences, 128
Yale Journal on Regulation, 132

HOSPITALS
Health Administration: Laws Regulations [KF 3821], 175
Health Care Labor Manual [KF 3580], 175
HEALTH PLANNING & ADMINISTRATION, 90
Hospital Cost Management [RA 971], 175

HOUSING
Census of Population and Housing, 40
Condemnation Procedures & Techniques [KF 5599], 169
Condominium Law & Practice [KF 581], 170
Cooperative Housing Law & Practice [KF 623], 170
Equal Opportunity in Housing [KF 5740], 172
Fair Housing-Fair Lending [KF 5740], 172

Government Reports
Announcement & Index, 75
Housing & Development
Reporter [KF 5726], 176

INDEXING SERVICES
Accountant's Index, 96
Alternative Press Index, 96
Bibliographic Index, 63
CSI/Federal Index, 96
Current Law Index, 97
General Periodical Index, 97
Index to Current Urban
Documents, 97
Index to Legal Periodicals, 98
Index to Periodical Articles
Related to Law, 98
Index to U.S Government
Periodicals, 98
Legal Resource Index, 98
PAIS Bulletin, 99
Shepard's Law Review
Citations, 99
Social Science Citation Index,
100
Social Science Index, 99

INSURANCE
SPECIAL LIBRARIES
ASSOCIATION, 203
Unemployment Insurance
Reports [KF 3673], 182

**INTERGOVERNMENTAL
COOPERATION**
ACIR, 189
Intergovernmental Perspective,
189
State Government: CQ's Guide,
18

INTERNATIONAL ORGANIZATIONS
Congressional Directory, 5
Federal Staff Directory, 9
United States Government
Manual, 10, 210

**JOURNAL INDEXES (see
INDEXING SERVICES)**

**JUDICIAL OFFICIALS (see also
COURTS)**
Congressional Directory, 5
CQ's Guide to the U.S.
Supreme Court, 17
Federal-State-Local
Government Directory, 4
Martindale-Hubbell Law
Directory, 21
State Elective Officials and the
Legislatures, 12
Taylor's Encyclopedia of
Government Officials, 4
United States Government
Manual, 10, 210

LABOR RELATIONS
BNA (Bureau of National
Affairs) (202)452-7889, 183
Collective Bargaining
Negotiations [KF 3408], 169
Directory of Labor Relations
[KF 3421], 171
Employment Practices Guide
[KF 3464], 171
FEDERAL REGISTER
ABSTRACTS, 148
Government Employee
Relations Report [KF 3580],
174
Health Care Labor Manual [KF
3580], 175
Human Resources
Management [KF 3455], 176
ICPERS, 149
Industrial Relations Guide [KF
3366], 176
Labor Arbitration Awards [KF
9085], 176
Labor Arbitration Index [KF
3421.5], 176
Labor Relations Reporter [KF
3314], 177
LABORLAW, 150, 177
NLRB Case Handling Manual
[KF 3372], 178
P-H (Prentice-Hall)
(800)223-0231, 183

Personnel Management Abstracts, 92

Personnel Management [KF 3365], 178

Policy & Practice Series [KF 3812 or KF 3788], 178

Public Employee Bargaining [KF 3409], 179, 180

LABOR RELATIONS (JOURNALS)

Employee Benefit Plan Review, 107

From the State Capitals. Public Employee Policy, 110

Government Union Review, 111

Human Resources Abstracts, 91

Journal of Collective Negotiations in the Public Sector, 114

Personnel Management Abstracts, 92

LABOR UNIONS

Employee and Union Member Guide to Labor Law [KF 3369], 171

National Trade and Professional Associations, 25, 188, 208

Washington Information Directory, 5

LAW

CONGRESSIONAL RECORD ABSTRACTS, 148

CSI Federal Index, 96

Encyclopedia of the American Constitution, 60

Facts on File Dictionary of Public Administration, 60

Fundamentals of Legal Research, 69

How to Find the Law, 69, 218

LEXIS, 150

NATIONAL ASSOCIATION OF ATTORNEYS GENERAL, 198

NATIONAL CENTER FOR STATE COURTS, 199

Public Administration Dictionary, 61

Reporter's Handbook, 78

Searching the Law, 69, 221

United States Law Week [KF 105], 167

WESTLAW, 150

LAW (JOURNALS)

Administrative Law Review, 101

American Business Law Journal, 102

Columbia Journal of Law and Social Problems, 105

Current Law Index, 97

Harvard Civil Rights/Civil Liberties Law Review, 112

Index to Legal Periodicals, 98

Index to Periodical Articles Related to Law, 98

Industrial Relations Law Journal, 113

Journal of Health Politics, Policy and Law, 115

Law & Society Review, 117

Law and Policy, 118

Legal Resource Index, 98

National Contract Management Journal, 120

Northwestern University Law Review, 121

Public Contract Law Journal, 124

School Law Bulletin (Boston), 127

Shepard's Law Review Citations, 99

Southern California Law Review, 128

University of Detroit Law Review, 130

Urban Law and Policy, 131

Urban Lawyer, 131

Yale Journal on Regulation, 132

LAW ENFORCEMENT

Criminal Justice Abstracts, 115-116, 128

Municipal Year Book, 14, 187, 208

State Policy Data Book, 41

LAW ENFORCEMENT (JOURNALS)
Journal of Police Science and
Administration, 115
Journal of Research in Crime
and Delinquency, 116
Law and Policy, 118
Law and Society Review, 117
Social Forces, 127

LAWYERS
AMERICAN BAR
ASSOCIATION, 191
Law and Business Directory of
Corporate Counsel, 21
Martindale-Hubbell Law
Directory, 21
Washington Lobbyists &
Lawyers Directory, 22

LEGAL INFORMATION SERVICES
BNA (Bureau of National
Affairs) (202)452-7889, 183
Callaghan & Co.
(800)323-1336, 183
CCH (Commerce Clearing
House) (312)583-8500, 183
Legal Looseleafs in Print, 167
LEXIS, 150
Mead Data Central (800)
346-9759, 142
P-H (Prentice-Hall)
(800)223-0231, 183
United States Law Week [KF
105], 167
WESTLAW, 150
West Publishing Company
(800) 328-9352, 144

LEGISLATION
CIS/INDEX, 147
Columbia Journal of Law and
Social Problems, 105
Congress and the Nation, 17
Congressional Index, 15, 167
CQ Almanac, 15
CQ Weekly Report, 15
CONGRESSIONAL RECORD
ABSTRACTS, 148
Editorial Research Reports, 107
Nation's Cities Weekly, 119

National Journal, 120
United States Government
Manual, 10, 210

LEGISLATIVE PROCESS
CIS/INDEX, 147
Congressional Index, 15, 167
LABORLAW, 150
LEXIS, 150
WESTLAW, 150

**LEGISLATIVE RESEARCH
BUREAUS**
Directory of Organizations and
Individuals, 20
State Legislative Leadership,
12, 209

LIBRARIES
Census Catalog and Guide, 29
Directory of Federal Libraries,
71
Directory of Government
Document Collections &
Librarians, 71
Guide to State Legislative
Materials [KF 1], 175
Introduction to U.S. Public
Documents, 77
SPECIAL LIBRARIES
ASSOCIATION, 203
State Legislative Leadership,
12, 209
Subject Collections, 70
Tapping the Government
Grapevine, 80

LOBBYING
Almanac of American Politics,
3, 205
Federal-State-Local
Government Directory, 4
Handbook of State Legislative
Leaders, 11
National Directory of Corporate
Public Affairs, 21
Politics in America, 9
State Legislative Sourcebook,
82
Tax Exempt Organizations [KF
6449], 172, 182

Washington Lobbyists &
Lawyers Directory, 22
Washington Representatives, 22

LOCAL GOVERNMENT
Problem-Solving for State and
Local Government, 90
ACIR, 189
AMERICAN ASSOCIATION OF
SMALL CITIES, 190
City Government Finances, 43
Compendium of Government
Finances, 45
Country and City Finance
Data, 156
County and City Data Book,
42, 206
County Executive Directory, 13
Current Municipal Problems,
206
Directory of City Policy
Officials, 13
Federal-State-Local
Government Directory, 4
Finances of County
Government, 45
Finances of Municipal and
Township Governments, 45
Finances of Public School
Systems, 45
Finances of Special Districts, 45
Financing State and Local
Governments, 48
FYI...; Resources on Local
Government, 1983-85, 216
Government Employment, 45
Government Organization, 45
Governmental Finances, 45
Guide to Audits of Local
Governments, 48
Guide to Municipal Official
Statements [KF 5315], 174
Guide to the Census of
Governments, 46
Index to Current Urban
Documents, 84-85, 97

INTERNATIONAL
ASSOCIATION OF
MUNICIPAL CLERKS, 196,
197
INTERNATIONAL CITY
MANAGEMENT
ASSOCIATION, 197
INTERNATIONAL MUNICIPAL
SIGNAL ASSOCIATION, 197
Local Government Finances in
Major County Areas, 44
Local Government in
Metropolitan Areas, 45
Local Government Law [KF
5300], 177
Municipal Executive Directory,
13
Municipal Government
Reference Sources, 85
Municipal Ordinances [KF
5313], 177
Municipal Year Book, 14, 187,
208
Municipal/County Executive
Directory, 13
NATIONAL ASSOCIATION OF
COUNTIES, 198
NATIONAL CIVIC LEAGUE, 199
National Directory of
Newsletters, 110
NATIONAL LEAGUE OF
CITIES, 201
PUBLIC TECHNOLOGY, 202
State and Local Government
Political Dictionary, 62
State and Metropolitan Area
Data Book, 42
Taxable Property Values and
Assessment, 45
Topical Studies, 45
UNITED STATES
CONFERENCE OF MAYORS,
203

**LOCAL GOVERNMENT
(JOURNALS)**
Problem-Solving Information,
90
American City & County, 103

Baseline Data Report, 104
City Almanac, 105
City Hall Digest, 105
Current Municipal Problems, 107
Government Executive, 110
Government Finance Review, 110
M I S (Management Information Service) Report, 119
National Civic Review, 120
Nation's Cities Weekly, 119
NLC Washington Report to the Nations Cities, 121
Public Management, 124
State and Local Government Review, 129
Urban Lawyer, 131
Ways & Means, 132

LOCAL GOVERNMENT DATA (see also STATISTICS)
Annual Survey of Government Finances, 43-44
Baseline Data Reports, 93
Country and City Finance Data, 157
Municipal Year Book, 14, 187, 208 MACHINE-READABLE DATA (see also

CD-ROM)
BLS Data Diskettes, 157
Census Catalog and Guide, 158
Country and City Finance Data, 157
DataPro Directory of On-Line Services, 160
Encyclopedia of Information Systems and Services, 161
Federal Statistical Data Bases, 157

MAILING LISTS
Direct Mail Lists Rates and Data, 26

MANAGEMENT
AMA Management Handbook, 59

AMERICAN SOCIETY FOR PUBLIC ADMINISTRATION, 193
Business Information Sources, 68, 214
Encyclopedia of Management, 60
National Technical Information Service, 91
NTIS, 91
Sources of Information in the Social Sciences, 64

MANAGEMENT (JOURNALS)
Administration and Management, 90
Current Municipal Problems, 107
Group and Organization Studies, 112
Harvard Business Review, 112
Journal of Management, 115
Management World, 118
National Contract Management Journal, 120
Parks and Recreation, 121
Public Administration Quarterly, 122
Public Administration Review, 123
Public Management, 124
Public Personnel Management, 125
Public Productivity Review, 125
Review of Public Personnel Administration, 126
State Government, 129

MAYORS
Directory of City Policy Officials, 13
Municipal Executive Directory, 13
Washington Information Directory, 5

MILITARY
INDEX TO U.S. GOVERNMENT PERIODICALS, 149

MUNICIPAL GOVERNMENT (see LOCAL GOVERNMENT)

NEWSLETTERS
From the State Capitals, 110
National Directory of Newsletters, 110
NewsNet, 143
Wakeman-Walworth, Inc. (703) 549-8606, 110

NEWSPAPER INDEXES
NEWSEARCH, 151
VU/TEXT, 143, 151

NEWSPAPERS
Congressional Directory, 5
Federal-State-Local Government Directory, 4
Literary Market Place, 72
UPI NEWS, 151
VU/TEXT, 143

NON-GOVERNMENTAL ORGANIZATIONS
Federal Staff Directory, 9
Washington Information Directory, 5

NOT FOR PROFIT ORGANIZATIONS
Business Information Sources, 214
Charitable Giving and Solicitation [KF 6388], 182
Encyclopedia of Associations, 24
Exempt Organizations Reporter [KF 6449], 172
Inventory of Data Sources, 159
National Trade and Professional Associations, 25, 188, 208
Tax Exempt Organizations [KF 6449], 182

NOT FOR PROFIT ORGANIZATIONS (JOURNALS)
Journal of Volunteer Administration, 117
Social Science Quarterly, 127

OFFICE MANAGEMENT (JOURNALS)
Bureaucrat, 104
Government Finance Review, 110
Management World, 118
Public Management, 124
Public Personnel Management, 125

ONLINE DATABASES (see also ABSTRACTING SERVICES, LAW, etc.)
ASI, 33
BOOKS IN PRINT, 72
ENCYCLOPEDIA OF ASSOCIATIONS, 24
FOUNDATION DIRECTORY, 67
FOUNDATION GRANTS INDEX, 68
GPO PUBLICATIONS REFERENCE FILE, 79
NATIONAL FOUNDATIONS, 67
NEXIS, 142
ULRICH'S, 73

ONLINE DATABASES, DIRECTORIES AND GUIDES
Census Catalog and Guide, 158
Database Directory, 160
DATABASE OF DATABASES, 160
DataPro Directory of On-Line Services, 160
Directory of Online Databases, 160
Encyclopedia of Information Systems and Services, 161
Federal Database Finder, 37
Federal Statistical Data Bases, 38, 157

ONLINE SEARCHING
Manual of Online Search Strategies, 161
Online Database Search Services Directory, 161

ONLINE SERVICES
BRS Information Technologies (800) 345-4277, 140

CompuServe (800) 848-8199, 140

Dialog Information Services (800) 334-2564, 141

EasyNet (800) 841-9553, 141

Encyclopedia of Information Systems and Services, 161

H.W. Wilson Company (800) 367-6770, 144

Mead Data General (800) 346-9759, 142

NewsNet (800) 345-1301, 143

Online Database Search Services Directory, 161

VU/TEXT (800) 258-8080, 143

West Publishing Company (800) 328-9352, 144

ONLINE SERVICES (JOURNALS)
Database, 162
Online, 162
Online Review, 162

ORGANIZATIONAL CHARTS
Guide to Public Administration, 217
United States Government Manual, 10, 210

PENSIONS
Pension Plan Guide [KF 736], 178
Pension Reporter [KF 3510], 178
Social Security Bulletin, 127

PEOPLE
Almanac of American Politics, 3, 205
Community Resources Directory, 23
Congressional Directory, 5
Congressional Index, 15
Congressional Staff Directory, 6
Congressional Yellow Book, 6
Consultants and Consulting Organizations Directory, 19
County Executive Directory, 13
Directory of City Policy Officials, 13

Directory of Government Document Collections & Librarians, 71

Directory of Organizations and Individuals, 20

Directory of Staff Assistants to the Governors, 10

Dun's Consultants Directory, 20

Encyclopedia of Governmental Advisory Organizations, 7

Federal Executive Directory, 7

Federal Regulatory Directory, 8

Federal Staff Directory, 9

Federal Statistical Directory, 30

Federal Yellow Book, 9

Federal-State-Local Government Directory, 4

Handbook of State Legislative Leaders, 11

Minority Consultants, 20

Municipal Executive Directory, 13

Municipal Year Book, 14, 187, 208

Municipal/County Executive Directory, 13

National Directory of Corporate Public Affairs, 21

National Directory of State Agencies, 11

Politics in America, 9

Research Services Directory, 20

State Administrative Officials, 11

State Elective Officials and the Legislatures, 12

State Legislative Leadership, 12, 209

Taylor's Encyclopedia of Government Officials, 4

United States Government Manual, 10, 210

Washington Information Directory, 5

Washington Lobbyists & Lawyers Directory, 22

Washington Representatives, 22

PERSONAL INCOME
Almanac of the 50 States, 39
Census of Population and
Housing, 40
Detailed Population
Characteristics, 41
Economic Indicators, 50
Economic Report of the
President, 47
Federal Reserve Bulletin, 50
General Social and Economic
Characteristics, 41
Governmental Finances, 44
State Government Finances, 44

**PERSONNEL (see also LABOR
RELATIONS)**
HRIN (Human Resource
Information Network), 146
ICPERS, 149
LABORLAW, 150
Labor Arbitration Index [KF
3421.5], 176

PERSONNEL (JOURNALS)
Administration and Society, 101
Administrative Science
Quarterly, 102
American Review of Public
Administration, 104
Bureaucrat, 104
Government Executive, 110
Group and Organization
Studies, 112
Human Communication
Research, 112
Human Resources Abstracts,
91
International Journal of Public
Administration, 113
Monthly Labor Review, 119
Personnel Management
Abstracts, 92
Psychological Abstracts, 92-93
Public Administration
Quarterly, 122
Public Management, 124
Public Personnel Management,
125

Public Productivity Review, 125
Review of Public Personnel
Administration, 126
Work and Occupations, 132

PERSONNEL MANAGEMENT
AMA Management Handbook,
59
Business Information Sources,
68, 214
Collective Bargaining
Negotiations [KF 3408], 169
Employee Benefits Cases
Service [KF 3315], 171
Employment Safety & Health
Guide [KF 3568.4], 171
EEO Compliance Manual [KF
3464], 172
Federal Employment Relations
Manual [KF 3409], 173
Government Reports
Announcement & Index, 75
Handbook of Human
Resources Administration, 61
Human Resources
Management [KF 3455], 176
Labor Relations Reporter [KF
3314], 177
LABORLAW, 177
Negotiated Employee Benefit
Plans [KF 3510], 178
Personnel Management [KF
3365], 178
Policy & Practice Series [KF
3812 or KF 3788], 178
Public Personnel
Administration [KF 3580],
180

**PLANNING (see also URBAN
AFFAIRS, ZONING)**
AMERICAN PLANNING
ASSOCIATION, 192
National Technical Information
Services, 91
NTIS, 91
Social Planning, Policy and
Development Abstracts, 93

PLANNING (JOURNALS)
Environment and Planning, 108
Evaluation and Program
Planning, 108
HEALTH PLANNING &
ADMINISTRATION, 90
Journal of the American
Planning Association, 117
Land Use and Zoning Digest,
117
Sage Urban Studies Abstracts,
93
Social Planning, Policy and
Development Abstracts, 93
Socio-Economic Planning
Sciences, 128

POLICY STUDIES (JOURNALS)
Human Resources Abstracts,
91
Policy Studies Review, 122
Polity, 122

POLITICAL PARTIES
Almanac of American Politics,
3, 205
CQ Almanac, 15
CQ Weekly Report, 15
CQ's Guide to U.S. Elections,
54
Federal-State-Local
Government Directory, 4
Politics in America, 9
State Elective Officials and the
Legislatures, 12

POLITICAL SCIENCE
Information Sources of Political
Science, 219
Sources of Information in the
Social Sciences, 64

POLITICAL SCIENCE (JOURNALS)
Administrative Science
Quarterly, 102
American Journal of Political
Science, 103
American Political Science
Review, 103
Annals, 102

Congress and the Presidency,
106
CQ Service. Weekly Report, 106
Legislative Studies Quarterly,
118
National Journal, 120
Policy Studies Journal, 121
Policy Studies Review, 122
Political Science Quarterly, 122
Polity, 122
Public Administration Review,
123
Publius, 126
Social Science Citation Index,
100
Social Science Index, 99
State Legislatures, 129
United States Political Science
Documents, 95

POLITICS
Almanac of American Politics,
3, 205
American Political Dictionary,
59
Congress and the Nation, 17
CQ Almanac, 15
CQ Weekly Report, 15
Current Events Transcripts
Service, 16
Federal-State-Local
Government Directory, 4
Safire's Political Dictionary, 61
State Legislative Sourcebook,
82
Vital Speeches of the Day, 16

PRIVATIZATION
ABI/INFORM, 89
Government Contracts
Reporter [KF 846], 174
Journal of Economic
Literature, 91
Social Science Quarterly, 127
Social Service Review, 128

PSYCHOLOGY (JOURNALS)
Environment and Behavior, 108
Human Communication
Research, 112

Journal of Research in Crime and Delinquency, 116
Journal of Social Issues, 116
Psychological Abstracts, 92
PsycINFO, 92
Social Science Index, 99

PUBLIC ADMINISTRATION PROFESSION
AMERICAN SOCIETY FOR PUBLIC ADMINISTRATION, 193
Guide to the Foundations of Public Administration, 217
Public Administration Times, 193

PUBLIC EMPLOYMENT (see also FEDERAL EMPLOYMENT)
Book of the States, 39, 206
ICPERS, 149
Municipal Year Book, 14, 187, 208

PUBLIC FINANCE (see also BONDS, ECONOMIC INDICATORS, FINANCE)
Almanac of American Politics, 3, 205
Almanac of the 50 States, 39
Annual Survey of Government Finances, 43
ASSOCIATION OF GOVERNMENT ACCOUNTANTS, 194
Book of the States, 39, 206
Budget of the U.S. Government, 47
Census of Governments, 45
City Government Finances, 43
Compendium of Government Finances, 45
County Government Finances, 43
Economic Indicators, 50
Facts and Figures on Government Finance, 46, 207
Federal Reserve Bulletin, 50
Finances of County Government, 45

Finances of Municipal and Township Governments, 45
Finances of Public School Systems, 45
Finances of Special Districts, 45
Financing State and Local Governments, 48
GOVERNMENT FINANCE OFFICERS ASSOCIATION, 195
Governmental Finances, 44, 45
Guide to Audits of Local Governments, 48
Guide to the Census of Governments, 46
Local Government Finances in Major County Areas, 44
Local Government in Metropolitan Areas, 45
Moody's Municipal and Government Manual, 48
Public Administration Dictionary, 61
Public Finance: An Information Sourcebook, 48, 220
PUBLIC SECURITIES ASSOCIATION, 202
Significant Features of Fiscal Federalism, 46
Standard & Poor's Bond Guide, 48
State Government Finances, 44
State Government Reference Publications, 82
State Government Tax Collections, 44
State Policy Data Book, 41
Taxable Property Values and Assessment, 45
Topical Studies, 45
United States Budget in Brief, 47

PUBLIC OPINION
American Public Opinion Data, 55
American Public Opinion Index, 55
Gallup Report, 55

Guide to Resources and
Services, 55, 158
Public Opinion, 56
Public Opinion Quarterly, 56

PUBLIC POLICY
Congress and the Nation, 17
Congressional Index, 15
CQ Almanac, 15
CQ Weekly Report, 15
Current Events Transcripts
Service, 16
Federal-State-Local
Government Directory, 4
Guide to the Foundations of
Public Administration, 217
National Directory of State
Agencies, 11
Public Administration
Dictionary, 61
State Government: CQ's Guide,
18
State Policy Reports, 18
Vital Speeches of the Day, 16

PUBLIC RELATIONS
AMA Management Handbook,
59

PUBLIC WELFARE
ACIR, 189
Catalog of Federal Domestic
Assistance, 66
Federal Register, 66
Government Programs and
Projects Directory, 24
Protection of Abused Victims
[KF 9320], 179
State Policy Data Book, 41
Unemployment Insurance
Reports [KF 3673], 182

PUBLIC WORKS
AMERICAN PUBLIC WORKS
ASSOCIATION, 192

PUBLIC WORKS (JOURNALS)
American City & County, 103
Government Product News, 111
Nation's Cities Weekly, 119
Public Roads, 125

Public Utilities Fortnightly, 125
Public Works, 126
Survey of Current Business,
130

PUBLISHING
Books in Print, 72
Forthcoming Books, 72
Irregular Serials & Annuals, 73
Literary Market Place, 72
Standard Periodical Directory,
73
ULRICH'S, 73
Ulrich's International
Periodicals Directory, 73

RECREATION
FEDERAL REGISTER
ABSTRACTS, 148

RECREATION (JOURNALS)
Government Product News, 111
Parks and Recreation, 121

REGULATION
Administrative Practice Manual
[KF 5406], 168
Air & Water Pollution Control
[KF 3775], 168
Condemnation Procedures &
Techniques [KF 5599], 169
CSI Federal Index, 96
Environment Reporter [KF
3775], 172
FEDERAL REGISTER
ABSTRACTS, 148
Federal Regulatory Directory, 8
Government Contracts
Reporter [KF 846], 174
Guide to Public
Administration, 217
Health Administration: Laws
Regulations [KF 3821], 175
Pollution Control Guide [KF
3775], 179
Public Administration
Dictionary, 61
Securities Regulation & Law
Report [KF 1439], 180
Tapping the Government
Grapevine, 80

Zoning & Land Use Controls [KF 5698], 182

REGULATION (JOURNALS)
Law and Policy, 118
National Journal, 120
Yale Journal on Regulation, 132

REGULATORY AGENCIES
Administrative Practice Manual [KF 5406], 168
Federal Regulatory Directory, 8

RESEARCH CENTERS
Directory of Organizations and Individuals, 20
Government Programs and Projects Directory, 24
Government Research Centers Directory, 25
PUBLIC TECHNOLOGY, 202
Research Centers Directory, 70
Research Services Directory, 20
State Government Research Directory, 70

RETIREMENT SYSTEMS
Employee Benefits Compliance Coordinator [KF 736], 171
Negotiated Employee Benefit Plans [KF 3510], 178
Pension Plan Guide [KF 736], 178
Pension Reporter [KF 3510], 178
Topical Studies, 45

REVENUES (see also PUBLIC FINANCE)
Annual Survey of Government Finances, 43
Budget of the U.S. Government, 47
City Government Finances, 43
County Government Finances, 43
Governmental Finances, 44
Local Government Finances in Major County Areas, 44
Public Finance: An Information Sourcebook, 220

Significant Features of Fiscal Federalism, 46
State Government Finances, 44
State Government Tax Collections, 44

RURAL AFFAIRS (JOURNALS)
Journal of Human Resources, Education, Manpower, 115
Parks and Recreation, 121
Rural Sociology, 126
Social Forces, 127
Socio-Economic Planning Sciences, 128

SAFETY
ASSOCIATED PUBLIC-SAFETY COMMUNICATIONS OFFICERS, 190
Consumer Product Safety Guide [KF 1606], 170
Employment Safety & Health Guide [KF 3568.4], 171
LABORLAW, 150
Occupational Safety & Health Reporter [KF 3568], 178
Products Liability Reporter [KF 1296], 179
Products Liability [KF 1296], 179

SAFETY (JOURNALS)
Journal of Community Health, 114
Journal of Health and Human Resources Administration, 114
Public Health Reports, 124
Work and Occupations, 132

SECURITIES (see also BONDS)
CCH (Commerce Clearing House) (312)583-8500, 183
Guide to Municipal Official Statements [KF 5315], 174

SOCIAL POLICY
NEWSEARCH, 151

SOCIAL POLICY (JOURNALS)
Alternative Press Index, 96
Columbia Journal of Law and Social Problems, 105

Contemporary Policy Issues, 106
Current Municipal Problems, 107
Environment and Behavior, 108
Environment and Planning, 108
Journal of Health Politics, Policy and Law, 115
Journal of Policy Analysis and Management, 116
Law and Policy, 118
Legal Resource Index, 98
Modern Times, 119
Policy Studies Journal, 121
Polity, 122
Psychological Abstracts, 92
PsycINFO, 93
Public Choice, 123
Public Health Reports, 124
Urban and Social Change Review, 131
Urban Law and Policy, 131
Ways & Means, 132

SOCIAL SERVICES (see also ASSISTANCE, GOVERNMENT)
Protection of Abused Victims [KF 9320], 179
Unemployment Insurance Reports [KF 3673], 182

SOCIAL SERVICES (JOURNALS)
Administration and Society, 101
Administration in Social Work, 101
Community Development Journal, 106
Current Municipal Problems, 107, 206
Journal of Community Health, 114
Journal of Health and Human Resources Administration, 114
Journal of Volunteer Administration, 117
Social Science Quarterly, 127
Social Security Bulletin, 127

Social Service Review, 128
Social Work, 128
Social Work Research & Abstracts, 94
Urban and Social Change Review, 131

SOCIOLOGY (JOURNALS)
Annals, 102
Community Development Journal, 106
Rural Sociology, 126
Social Forces, 127
Social Science Quarterly, 127
Socio-Economic Planning Sciences, 128
Sociological Abstracts, 94
Urban and Social Change Review, 131

SPECIAL INTEREST GROUPS (see LOBBYING)

SPEECHES AND STATEMENTS
Current Events Transcripts Service, 16
Historic Documents of 19--, 76
Vital Speeches of the Day, 16

STATE DATA CENTERS
Census Catalog and Guide, 29
Federal Statistical Directory, 30

STATE GOVERNMENT
ACIR, 189
Almanac of American Politics, 3, 205
Almanac of the 50 States, 39
Bibliography of State Bibliographies, 80
Book of the States, 39, 206
COUNCIL OF STATE GOVERNMENTS, 194
Directory of Staff Assistants to the Governors, 10
Federal-State-Local Government Directory, 4
Financing State and Local Governments, 48
Government Employment, 45
Government Organization, 45

Guide to State Legislative
 Materials, 81
Guide to the Census of
 Governments, 46
Handbook of State Legislative
 Leaders, 11
Monthly Checklist of State
 Publications, 81
NATIONAL ASSOCIATION FOR
 STATE INFORMATION
 SYSTEMS, 198
National Directory of
 Newsletters, 110, 133
National Directory of State
 Agencies, 11
NATIONAL GOVERNORS
 ASSOCIATION, 200
State Administrative Officials,
 11
State and Local Government
 Political Dictionary, 62
State and Metropolitan Area
 Data Book, 42
State Elective Officials and the
 Legislatures, 12
State Government Finances, 44
State Government Reference
 Publications, 82
State Government Research
 Checklist, 221
State Government Research
 Directory, 70
State Government Tax
 Collections, 44
State Government: CQ's Guide,
 18
State Legislative Leadership,
 12, 209
State Legislative Sourcebook,
 82
State Legislatures, 222
State Policy Data Book, 41
State Policy Reports, 18
Taylor's Encyclopedia of
 Government Officials, 4
Topical Studies, 45
Washington Information
 Directory, 5

STATE GOVERNMENT (JOURNALS)
 Problem-Solving Information,
 90
 California Journal, 105
 Journal of State Taxation, 117
 State and Local Government
 Review, 129
 State Government, 129
 State Government News, 129
 State Legislatures, 129
 State Policy Reports, 130
 Ways & Means, 132
STATE LAWS
 Guide to State Legislative
 Materials, 81, 175
 LEXIS, 150
 NATIONAL ASSOCIATION OF
 ATTORNEYS GENERAL, 198
 NATIONAL CONFERENCE ON
 UNIFORM STATE LAWS, 200
 Protection of Abused Victims
 [KF 9320], 179
 State Legislative Sourcebook,
 82
 Subject Compilations of State
 Laws, 84
 WESTLAW, 150
STATE LEGISLATURE
 Federal-State-Local
 Government Directory, 4
 Guide to State Legislative
 Materials, 81, 175
 Handbook of State Legislative
 Leaders, 11
 NATIONAL CONFERENCE OF
 STATE LEGISLATURES, 200
 State Elective Officials and the
 Legislatures, 12
 State Legislative Leadership,
 12, 209
 State Legislative Sourcebook,
 82
 State Legislatures, 222
 Taylor's Encyclopedia of
 Government Officials, 4

STATE MOTTOS
Taylor's Encyclopedia of Government Officials, 4

STATE SEALS
Taylor's Encyclopedia of Government Officials, 4

STATE TAXPAYERS ASSOCIATIONS
Directory of Organizations and Individuals, 20

STATISTICAL ACTIVITIES OF GOVERNMENT
Status of Major Federal Statistical Agencies, 35
Annual Survey of Government Finances, 43
Book of the States, 39, 206
Census and You, 36
Census of Governments, 45
City Government Finances, 43
Compendium of Government Finances, 45
Congress and the Nation, 17
CQ's Guide to Congress, 17
County and City Data Book, 42, 206
County Government Finances, 43
Facts and Figures on Government Finance, 46, 207
Federal Statistical Directory, 30
Federal Statistical System 1980 to 1985, 35
Federal-State-Local Government Directory, 4
Finances of County Government, 45
Finances of Municipal and Township Governments, 45
Finances of Public School Systems, 45
Finances of Special Districts, 45
Government Employment, 45
Governmental Finances, 44, 45
Guide to Statistical Materials, 31

Guide to the Census of Governments, 46
Historical Statistics of the United States, 40
Local Government Finances in Major County Areas, 44
Local Government in Metropolitan Areas, 45
Significant Features of Fiscal Federalism, 46
State Government Finances, 44
State Government Tax Collections, 44
State Policy Data Book, 41
Taxable Property Values and Assessment, 45
Topical Studies, 45

STATISTICAL TIME SERIES
Business Conditions Digest, 49
Conference Board, CBDB Data Disk, 156
Country and City Finance Data, 156
Economics Sourcebook of Government Statistics, 29
Facts and Figures on Government Finance, 46, 207
Handbook of Basic Economic Statistics, 51
Handbook of Labor Statistics, 51
Historical Statistics of the United States, 40
Significant Features of Fiscal Federalism, 46
Standard & Poor's Statistical Service, 52
Survey of Current Business, 52, 210

STATISTICS (JOURNALS)
American Demographics, 103
Federal Reserve Bulletin, 109
Monthly Labor Review, 119
Monthly Products Announcement, 36
Social Security Bulletin, 127

Survey of Current Business, 130

STATISTICS, AIDS AND GUIDES
American Statistical Index, 33
ASI, 33
Business Serials of the U.S. Government, 49
Census Catalog and Guide, 29
Directory of Computer Software, 37
Economics Sourcebook of Government Statistics, 29
Factfinder for the Nation, 30
Federal Information Sources in Health and Medicine, 216
Federal Statistical Data Bases, 38
Federal Statistical Directory, 30
Guide to Statistical Materials, 31
Guide to U.S. Government Statistics, 31
Handbook of U.S. Economic and Financial Indicators, 31
Locating U.S. Government Information, 77
Major Programs: Bureau of Labor Statistics, 32
Statistical Reference Index, 34
Statistics Sources, 32
Tapping the Government Grapevine, 80

STATISTICS, ECONOMICS (see ECONOMIC INDICATORS, EMPLOYMENT, FINANCE, etc.)

STATISTICS, INDEXES
American Statistical Index, 33
ASI, 33
Statistical Reference Index, 34

STATISTICS, LABOR
Almanac of the 50 States, 39
BLS Data Diskettes, 157
Detailed Population Characteristics, 41
Economic Indicators, 50
Economic Report of the President, 47, 207

Federal Reserve Bulletin, 50
General Social and Economic Characteristics, 41
Government Employment, 45
Handbook of Labor Statistics, 51
Historical Statistics of the United States, 40
Major Programs: Bureau of Labor Statistics, 32
Monthly Labor Review, 51
Standard & Poor's Statistical Service, 52
State Policy Data Book, 41
Statistical Abstract of the United States, 42, 209
Survey of Current Business, 52, 210

STATISTICS, POLICIES
Federal Statistical System 1980 to 1985, 35
Guide to the Census of Governments, 46
Statistical Policy Handbook, 35
Status of Major Federal Statistical Agencies, 35

STATISTICS, PUBLIC OPINION
American Public Opinion Data, 55
American Public Opinion Index, 55
Gallup Report, 55
Guide to Resources and Services, 55
Public Opinion, 56
Public Opinion Quarterly, 56

STATISTICS, SOURCES OF
ACIR, 189
Almanac of the 50 States, 39
Annual Survey of Government Finances, 43
Book of the States, 39, 206
Business Conditions Digest, 49
Census Catalog and Guide, 29
Census of Governments, 45
Census of Population and Housing, 40

City Government Finances, 43

Compendium of Government Finances, 45

Congressional District Data Book, 41

County and City Data Book, 42, 206

County Government Finances, 43

CPI Detailed Report, 50

Detailed Population Characteristics, 41

Economic Indicators, 50

Economics Sourcebook of Government Statistics, 29

Facts and Figures on Government Finance, 46, 207

Federal Reserve Bulletin, 50

Finances of County Government, 45

Finances of Municipal and Township Governments, 45

Finances of Public School Systems, 45

Finances of Special Districts, 45

Financing State and Local Governments, 48

General Social and Economic Characteristics, 41

Government Employment, 45

Government Organization, 45

Governmental Finances, 44, 45

Handbook of Labor Statistics, 51

Handbook of U.S. Economic and Financial Indicators, 31

Historical Statistics of the United States, 40

Local Government Finances in Major County Areas, 44

Local Government in Metropolitan Areas, 45

Monthly Labor Review, 51

Significant Features of Fiscal Federalism, 46

Social Security Bulletin, 127

Standard & Poor's Statistical Service, 52

State and Metropolitan Area Data Book, 42

State Government Finances, 44

State Government Tax Collections, 44

State Policy Data Book, 41

Statistical Abstract of the United States, 42, 209

Taxable Property Values and Assessment, 45

Topical Studies, 45

U.S. Industrial Outlook, 53

World Almanac and Book of Facts, 64, 211

SUPREME COURT

CQ Almanac, 15

CQ's Guide to the U.S. Supreme Court, 17

United States Law Week [KF 105], 167

TAX POLICY

Public Finance: An Information Sourcebook, 220

TAXATION

ACIR, 189

All-States Tax Reports [KF 1670], 169

CCH (Commerce Clearing House) (312)583-8500, 183

Comparative State Income Tax Guide [KF 6752], 169

Facts and Figures on Government Finance, 46, 207

FEDERAL REGISTER ABSTRACTS, 148

Federal Tax Articles [KF 6335], 173

Federal Taxation [KF 6335], 173

Financing State and Local Governments, 48

INTERNATIONAL ASSOCIATION OF ASSESSING OFFICERS, 196

LEXIS, 150

Public Finance: An Information Sourcebook, 220
RIA (Research Institute of America) (800)431-2057, 183
Sales Taxes [KF 1670], 180
Significant Features of Fiscal Federalism, 46
State and Local Taxes [KF 6750], 181
State Government Tax Collections, 44
State Tax Action Coordinator [KF 6750], 181
State Tax Guide [KF 6750], 181
State Tax Reports [KF 1670], 181
Tax Exempt Organizations [KF 6449], 172, 182
Taxable Property Values and Assessment, 45
WESTLAW, 150

TAXATION (JOURNALS)
Environment and Planning, 108
Government Finance Review, 110
National Tax Journal, 120

TELEVISION
Congressional Directory, 5
Federal-State-Local Government Directory, 4
Literary Market Place, 72

TOURIST GUIDES
State Government Reference Publications, 82

TRADE AND INDUSTRY (see also BUSINESS, ECONOMIC INDICATORS)
National Trade and Professional Associations, 25, 188, 208

TRAINING AND DEVELOPMENT
Community Resources Directory, 23
Employment and Training Reporter [KF 3775], 171
Training and Development Organizations Directory, 22

TRANSPORTATION
BNA (Bureau of National Affairs) (202)452-7889, 183
Government Reports Announcement & Index, 75
State Policy Data Book, 41

TRANSPORTATION (JOURNALS)
Public Roads, 125
Public Works, 126

URBAN AFFAIRS (see also LOCAL GOVERNMENT)
Index to Current Urban Documents, 84, 97
Municipal Government Reference Sources, 85
NATIONAL LEAGUE OF CITIES, 201
URBAN INSTITUTE, 204
Zoning & Land Use Controls [KF 5698], 182

URBAN AFFAIRS (JOURNALS)
Baseline Data Reports, 93
California Journal, 105
City Hall Digest, 105
Computers, Environment and Urban Systems, 106
Environment and Planning, 108
Journal of Urban Affairs, 117
Nation's Cities Weekly, 119
National Civic Review, 120
NLC Washington Report to the Nations Cities, 121
Public Administration Review, 123
Public Productivity Review, 125
Review of Public Personnel Administration, 126
Sage Urban Studies Abstracts, 93
Social Forces, 127
Southern California Law Review, 128
State and Local Government Review, 129
State Government News, 129
State Legislatures, 129

University of Detroit Law
Review, 130
Urban Affairs Quarterly, 131
Urban and Social Change
Review, 131
Urban Law and Policy, 131
Urban Lawyer, 131
Washington University
Journal, 132

VOLUNTEERS
Community Resources
Directory, 23
National Trade and
Professional Associations,
25, 188, 208
Social Science Quarterly, 127

VOTING STATISTICS
America Votes, 54
Book of the States, 39, 206
Congress and the Nation, 17
Congressional Index, 15
CQ Almanac, 15
CQ Weekly Report, 15
CQ's Guide to U.S. Elections,
54
Politics in America, 9
Statistical Abstract of the
United States, 42, 209

**WATER (see ENGINEERING,
ENVIRONMENT)**
ZONING
American Law of Zoning [KF
5698], 169
Zoning & Land Use Controls
[KF 5698], 183